The Friendly Gestapo Man

And Other Stories of My Life

by

Erwin Biener

January, 2012

The Friendly Gestapo Man

First Printing by First Choice Books, Canada
Second Printing By Digital Print Australia

Published by the Mickie Dalton Foundation
Australia

For information address: info@mickiedaltonfoundation.com

First Published in 2012 in Australia

ISBN: 978 0987 1675 76

Published by The Mickie Dalton Foundation
Kempsey, NSW
Australia

www.mickiedaltonfoundation.com

Dedication

This book is dedicated to the memory of my mother
Johanna ("Hansy") Biener

Acknowledgements.

This book would never have appeared without the help and continuous encouragement of Michael Davies. He saw this book through the publication process. He not only edited my vignettes but also designed the book cover. He also gave me *carte blanche* which greatly encouraged me in writing my vignettes and other pieces.

I owe special thanks to Pelle Nilsson, the host of the internet forum in which a number of my vignettes had appeared. I have followed his useful suggestion to include in my introduction an account of the historical background of the Holocaust in Hungary.

I also thank Judith Spencer who steadfastly encouraged me to publish my stories despite my doubts that they will ever reach a wider audience.

And last but not least, my thanks go to Mark Dakin, who, apart from solving a lot of computer problems, also scanned all the family pictures.

Contents

Introduction

I don't know why, but one evening many years ago, while scanning the memories thread of the Internet Forum "Table Talk," I had a sudden idea: why not share with other readers one of my most vivid experiences of the Second World War? Without any hesitation I started typing and out flowed a memory which I had never thought I would be able to record. Certainly, this wasn't a Proustian opening of the subconscious, a sudden "remembrance of things past." Rather, it was something quite inexplicable at least as this upsurge of memories is concerned. And even though the scene I was trying to put into words was gruesome in a strange way it also energized me, for I realized that I could dig deeper than I had imagined; and equally important, I had also realized that I could convey some of my experiences to the reader which I had never thought that I would be able to do.

A short time ago, the host of the thread where some of my vignettes have appeared raised a rather interesting question: "Am I right to assume that the relation between fact and fiction is something you grapple with in your current project?" He was referring to the vignettes which I was preparing for this book and whose truth value may be subject to doubt. I can only say that what I went through in the Holocaust and later in my youth is no invention. The things I described had really happened. What is in question however, are the many details which I have over the years forgotten. Similarly, I can only vaguely sense the varied atmospheres in which my experiences were couched. When they emerge, they take the forms of dreamlike residues of fugitive remembrances. They point to real episodes in my life which stand out against their blurred backgrounds. To make these experiences come alive I couldn't but tell a number of *stories*. By doing so I had to use my imagination to connect the many details and set the scene for the events which I was going to describe. In other words, I instinctively used the approach of the story-teller to give a sense of coherence and reality to my vignettes.

Even though the stories in this book give some idea of my origins and development, I would like to say something about my family background to fill the gaps in the vignettes.

I grew up as the only child of a well-to-do upper-middle class Jewish family. My father was a corporation lawyer and my mother a talented pianist. We lived in an unusually large apartment which overlooked the huge "Heroes Square," the parade ground of Budapest where foreign statesmen and other eminent international personalities laid down their wreaths at the foot of the heroes' monument. From the windows of our music room I could watch many of these colourful ceremonial occasions. I particularly remember the ascetic figure of Cardinal Pacelli (who later became Pope Pius XII) during the Eucharistic Congress in Budapest in 1938. And I can still hear the voice of grandpa Oscar shouting *"Viva la Papa."* More than anything else, I enjoyed the music of the military bands whose brassy sounds I loved to imitate no end.

There was a lot of music in our home. Mother as a pianist didn't only practice day after day, but also played a lot of chamber music with various string players fairly regularly. My parents used to have also musical evenings several times a year, which were preceded by a sumptuous dinner. Unfortunately, I was too young to participate in these *"soirées."* I knew, however, when they were taking place because my mother would wake me up on these days in the middle of the night to show off the "little master" to some of the admiring guests.

Following family tradition I became a student at the Lutheran grammar school of Budapest when I was eleven. This for me was an entirely new and formative experience because through the religious ethos of this school I was steeped in Protestant Baroque music, especially the chorals and organ works of J.S. Bach. Also, I became very familiar with the Lutheran liturgy and the New Testament which later helped me to pose as a Christian youngster when I had to go underground during the Holocaust.

I will never forget the day in 1943 when one evening, my mother suddenly said to me just before I was going to bed, “Erwin, they are killing the Jews in the East, they are shooting them by the thousands.” This was news to me because despite the war raging in Europe and elsewhere we still lived in unusual comfort as Jews, considering the anti-Semitism which was growing ever stronger in Hungary. We knew of course of the anti-Jewish legislations which had been legalized by the Hungarian Parliament. What’s more, we knew how very badly young Jewish men were treated who were forced into labour battalions and sent to the Eastern Front. They were given the most dangerous and humiliating jobs as slave workers of the Hungarian Army. As a member of an older generation my father had luckily, at least for the time being, escaped these horrors. He sensed the danger, especially when one of the guards of these battalions came to our house with the express intention of blackmailing him, hoping to extort money from a well-to-do Jew.

And then came March 19, 1944, the day when the German Army occupied Hungary. We knew pretty soon that the Nazi-appointed Hungarian government would do everything to make the lives of the Jews a living hell. Imitating the anti-Jewish program of the

Third Reich the Hungarian administration was bent on carrying out post haste with the help of their German allies, the "Final Solution." The destruction process set into motion by the so called "death bureaucrats" and carried out by the savage Jew-hating gendarmerie was, as the noted historian of the Holocaust Raoul Hilberg described it, based on a number of administrative measures. The first of these entailed the "definition," the application of the "Nuremberg Laws" according to which, the identity of the Jews was racially determined. The first, most tangible effect of these measures was the compulsory wearing of the Jewish star which had to be affixed to our breasts. While this inhuman measure deeply affected everyone who had to wear this ugly distinguishing mark, there was a group of Hungarian citizens who had specially felt the weight of this ugly ordinance. They were the men, women and children who were born or grew up as gentiles and who had until then, little or no connections with the Jewish faith or customs. As far as our family was concerned, father had us baptized when I was eight years old because he had hoped that becoming Lutherans we would be considered Christians rather than Jews. Now of course, as racially designated Jews, we had to carry the full brunt of the endless anti-Jewish regulations. As a result, my father was called up and had to join one of the slave labour units of the Hungarian Army and that's where he was murdered during the last months of the war. A short while after my father had left, mother and I had to leave our apartment and move into a so called "Jewish House." We found out only after the war that, according to official estimates,

> *"between late April and early July 1944 approximately 44,.000 Hungarian Jews were deported, around 426.000 of them to Auschwitz. The SS sent approximately 320,000 of them directly to the gas chambers in Auschwitz Birkenau."*

Most of these Jews were deported from the Hungarian provinces. We in Budapest would have been also sent there if the regent of Hungary, Admiral Miklos Horthy, hadn't prevented this final roundup of Jews destined for the gas chambers for purely political rather than humanitarian considerations. What happened to us there and how we managed to survive after we had gone underground is the subject of a number of my vignettes.

Like for so many other people our life after the war was quite difficult. Having lost her husband, my mother had to provide for us. But as she had neither the strength nor the means to do that for both of us, she sent me to a boarding school that cared for orphaned children. This was the remarkable foundation of the Lutheran reverend Gabor Sztehlo which became a Children's Republic called

"Gaudiopolis." The two years that I spent there profoundly affected my development. My stay there came to an end after the Communists, unable to tolerate such an enlightened educational project, put an end to this unique pedagogical experiment.

I felt very much lost in Communist Hungary. As a child of bourgeois parents, I had no chance to become a university student. However, had I become (or pretended to become like some of my classmates) an ardent Communist, I probably could have had the advantages of a higher education in Hungary. But as I hated to mouth Communist slogans and follow the party-line, my only wish was to escape to the West. After a failed attempt to sneak across the Iron Curtain, which had nearly cost my life, I had managed to flee to Austria with a number of companions, thanks to the help of a professional man-smuggler.

I still remember what Vienna looked like when I arrived there from the fortified Hungarian border on a bitterly cold January morning. There were still ruins everywhere and I saw a lot of American, English and French military personnel criss-crossing the city in their jeeps. It was the Vienna of the *"Third Man,"* the Vienna of that famous film classic, full of refugees and dubious characters working for various espionage agencies. Rather than lingering there, we slipped across the Soviet Zone of Austria and headed for Salzburg where my mother's sister and her husband lived. I had to spend part of the winter in Upper

Austria at a Jewish refugee camp, an experience which I described in one of my vignettes. Even though I had never expected that my mother would be able to flee Hungary, she too managed to escape to Austria with the help of another man-smuggler. A few months after her arrival in Salzburg, I moved with her to a picturesque village close to the city. As I was fluent in both German and English I got a job with one of the refugee organizations which saved us from moving to a refugee camp. However pleasant it was living near that beautiful city, we wanted to leave Europe at any price because we were terribly afraid of the possible international developments of the Cold War. Like many other people who escaped from Communist Eastern Europe, we were dreading the outbreak of another armed conflict. Thus I felt very lucky when in the spring of 1951, I received a visa as a "general labourer" to Canada. My mother, who had stayed behind waiting for an American visa had changed her mind after I promised to sponsor her as an immigrant. At first, she had a rather difficult time doing odd jobs in Canada until by a lucky stroke, she was able to work in her profession as a musician and a piano teacher. I too, had a very difficult start but eventually managed to save enough money to become a student at the University of Toronto.

My life took an unusual turn in 1958 when I decided to return to Europe to continue my studies in philosophy there. The four years I spent in England were quite challenging and interesting. I found the study of analytic philosophy rather difficult and yet rewarding because of its outspokenly linguistic approach which gave me a very good grounding in the shadings and complexities of the English language. I am certain that without this training I would never have been able to write, as a non-native speaker as clearly and concisely as possible.

Odd as it may appear, I decided to continue my graduate studies in Germany regardless of my love for the English language. But despite the fact that my facility in German lagged behind the way I spoke and wrote English, I decided to continue my training in Heidelberg because of my growing interests in certain branches of German philosophy. The time that I spent there and later in Frankfurt was both challenging and enriching. I was lucky enough to become a student of Jürgen Habermas, one of the most prominent contemporary philosophers. I was equally fortunate in my personal relationships for I have met a number of very interesting people, some of whom became my lifelong friends. While in Europe I made good use of travelling by *"autostop"* (hitch-hiking) that allowed me to see a good deal of France, and especially Paris "the city of light" which still fascinates me no end.

Having finished my thesis, I returned to Canada in 1967, after nearly nine years away from the country that I have learnt to love. My training in philosophy and my interests in the Fine Arts enabled me to find a position at a graduate school for teachers in Toronto. As a research associate I had got carte blanche to devise experimental courses for high-school students. What's more, my interests in Aesthetics allowed me to give graduate courses to teachers focusing on the relationship between the graphic arts and history with the help of an extensive slide-collection. I believe that this approach will enable teachers to devise new curricula with the aid of the visual arts, a method which, as I have found, stimulates both the students' reasoning and imagination.

After I retired I developed a great interest in the intriguing and manifold world of the Internet. I have particularly been drawn to the often boisterous and sometimes exasperating forums of the net which gave me a chance to develop my ideas and engage in discussions with a number of intelligent and enlightened participants. More than that, these electronic dialogues also gave me a chance to meet face-to-face a number of people from these forums in both the US and the Continent. Equally important, without the encouragement of a number of posters from various forums, I would never have dared to collect my vignettes and other pieces in the book that you are going to read.

Part 1

The Holocaust

The Boxer

Shortly after the Germans occupied Hungary, a good many Jewish students were forced by the Fascist Hungarian authorities to do forced labour. One day I was ordered to fill up huge bomb craters at the outskirts of Budapest with other fellow students. On another occasion, we were forced to go to one of the big cemeteries to fill sacks with straw for the Hungarian Army. When I stepped aside to take a short rest, one of the cemetery guards collared me and gave me a beating with a cane. This was my first encounter with a raging, violent anti-Semite and after that I knew that I could expect the same, if not worse.

Even though I was fortunate enough not to be physically harmed by these violent men, once I was the witness of a kind of abuse which is very difficult to forget.

As Protestant converts of an elite Protestant lycee, we were ordered one day into the offices of a para-military organization for young men. Fearing that we would be sent away to work as forced labourers, we were relieved to learn that we only had to fill out draft cards for Jewish students and deliver them to their addresses. While this wasn't an especially difficult job it was rather unpleasant. We had to visit houses at a run-down area of the city where the poorest Jews lived. This was the quarter of the Eastern Jews, the so called *"Galizianer,"* fairly recent immigrants from Poland or the border regions of Hungary who were largely unassimilated. Even though I often saw these Jews walking the streets in their distinctive caftans and broad-rimmed black hats, I had never had the occasion to make their acquaintance. And I had never desired to do so because we, belonging to the assimilated bourgeoisie, considered them as members of a strange tribe. What's more we were ashamed that we might be associated by the anti-Semites to these strange, ultra-orthodox men. In making my rounds with the draft cards, I entered many dark, dingy apartments reeking with strange odours coming from the kitchens. And I saw a lot of frightened people who probably considered me, even while I had to wear on my breast the distinctive yellow Jewish star, as a strange, if not evil messenger in the service of the murderous Hungarian authorities.

One day when we had to be again in the office I was told by one of my fellow students that they have seen B. around. He knew that he was not only a rabid anti-Semite but also a very violent man. He used to be a boxer who, thanks to his connections to extremist right-wing circles, had become an instructor of the para-military youth organization. A short while later, B. appeared. He was a stocky man with powerful shoulders who looked at us with a sardonic smile.

"Well, here you are, Jewboys. It seems that you can only sit on your asses day in day out. I am going to teach you a sport" he said. Pointing at two of the boys, he said, "You and you, come here."

I could see how frightened the two were because they expected something quite terrible from the instructor. To our surprise, he used neither his fists nor his feet. He simply told them to face each other at a very close distance.

"You," he said to the one student standing nearer to him. "Give your friend a good slap."

Nonplussed by this command the boy hesitated.

"Haven't you heard what I said, your dirty Jew," he shouted. "Hit him, if you don't do it, I am going to give you a good smack."

He was so threatening that the frightened student gave his classmate a very light smack. "That was nothing," B. roared. "Show him that you are a man," and he came quite close up to him.

The boy now hit the other one much more strongly.

"Now it is your turn," B. said to the other. "Give it to him back."

Frightened, the boy gave his "opponent" a fairly strong slap.

"This wasn't that bad," B. said. Pointing to the first boy, he said, "Now it's your turn again."

In a short while, the two students began to slap each other at regular intervals. As they went on, the slaps developed into fist fights. I had the impression that the two became really mad at each other as the "game" developed. At the end, they got really entangled. At this point, B. stopped the slapping-boxing match saying that this was irregular.

"Such close body contact is not allowed in the boxing arena," he said.

After the fight he turned to us. "I know that you are going to slaughter me like the Jew butchers the cattle, he growled. "But I will see to it that before then, I will bump off as many of you as I can."

Reading the newspaper a year after the war, I came upon a small item. It said that the Arrow Cross mass murderer B. had been executed. But while the sentence was being read out, he broke loose and set on the hangman and beat him up before he was overpowered by the guards.

In the Jewish House

In May 1944, two months after the Germans occupied Hungary, the Jews of Budapest were ordered to leave their houses and apartments and forced to move into the so called "Jewish Houses." This was the first step by the authorities to concentrate the Jews in specific dwellings; its purpose, to make the proposed deportation of the Jews to Auschwitz all the easier for the police and the gendarmes, which was planned to take place in one fell swoop early in July. I often wondered why we weren't taken immediately into a ghetto, as were most of the Jews in Eastern Europe prior to being transported in freight trains to the killing centers. This was done, I had learnt later, because the authorities believed that the allied bombers would spare the city if they knew that the Jewish houses were scattered all over Budapest. This was but wishful thinking considering the terrible bombing damage caused by American, British and Soviet airplanes, despite the fact that we were still living in the Jewish Houses.

I remember the day when we left our apartment in a horse cart with our necessities loaded in the back.

Sitting next to my mother beside the coachman, I was filled with apprehensions about the life at our new address. We were to move in to my aunt's and her second husband's apartment, two relatives whom I found always terribly unpleasant. He was a well to do, rather overbearing businessman, while his wife was a highly neurotic woman who was always jealous of my mother. What's more, she treated her son from her first marriage quite abominably, leaving him during these difficult times at the care of his rather fragile grandmother.

When we arrived we found the apartment packed with people. Aside from my mother's sister and her husband, his ancient parents were also crammed into the rooms as well as an unknown youngish woman who soon afterwards moved to another address.

Life in the Jewish House was a claustrophobic experience. We were under strict curfew, allowed only three hours in the early afternoon to go out to do our shopping. Even so, there was the danger of being arbitrarily collared by the police and deported out from the city to one of the internment camps. From there, the road left mostly to Auschwitz or other death factories. Despite these constricting conditions, I had tried to do the best I could in that big apartment building. I took the initiative to go down in the afternoons to one of the big boulevards and buy up a bunch of evening papers for the tenants of the house which I sold for a profit. This gave me sufficient pocket money to buy a few books and a nice fountain pen. I also met regularly a number of people, to some of whom I became quite attached. My uncle, however, was strictly against visiting my friends and acquaintances in the building.

"There aren't to be any visits to the neighbours", he said without giving any reasons for his ban.

Gradually, I had realized that this man was gunning for me. One day, for instance, he sent me to a barber in the house for a "smart haircut." I haven't sat for more than a few minutes in the master's chair when I noticed that, using a special electric clipper, he was cutting me bald. I looked like a prisoner from a special penal unit and I am sure that my uncle greatly enjoyed my appearance.

On another occasion after accusing me without the slightest grounds, for having left open the door of the fridge, he took his cane and gave me a terrible hiding. I felt very glad after he was taken away with men and women of his age-group by the police. (He and his wife were marched to the Austrian border, but both he and his wife managed to escape and survived the war).

There were terrible air raids during the summer. One day in early July, our house was hit during the carpet bombing by American Flying Fortresses. We remained buried for hours in the air raid shelter until we were finally dug out. One night, during another raid we noticed that my uncle's father was nowhere in the shelter. As no one made a move to bring down the old man, my mother suddenly got up and walked up to the fifth floor to lead him to the safety of the cellar. She later told me how difficult it was to drag down the old gentleman whose senses, weakened by dementia, seemed to be oblivious to the terrifying attack.

In mid October the extreme Fascist Arrow-Cross government took over the power. This "coup d'êtat" was the worst thing that could have happened to the Jews. Special units of this radical regime began to raid the Jewish Houses. These black-uniformed gangsters were often accompanied by policemen. Their objective was to select people belonging to a certain age group and send them marching on the highway toward the Austrian border - veritable death-marches for many people during the rainy, ice-cold November weather. Fearing that one day we might also be selected to join others in these deadly marches, we had decided to go underground.

One rainy day when we were already hiding out from the special units with the help of false papers as well as with the help of people who sheltered us, we noticed policemen and black uniformed members of the Arrow-Cross going in pairs in a certain direction.

Ignoring the significance of this obviously planned mobilization of repressive forces, my mother insisted on going back to the Jewish House to collect her umbrella. If I hadn't prevented her from entering our apartment we would have also have ended up on the highway. In fact, a few hours later everyone from our house was forced out into the street. They were first taken to an abandoned brickworks were forced to march like the others toward the Austrian border a day later.

I learnt after the war that an elderly doctor and his wife, whom I knew quite well, killed themselves rather than follow the others of the building in a death march in which they would surely have perished.

At the Nuntiatura
Budapest, November, 1944

Mother and I leave the Jewish house late in the afternoon. We had removed the star from our overcoats because we are going to take an illegal trip. We are heading for the Castle District on the other side of the Danube to obtain the so-called Vatican protective passport, our only hope of escaping the marauding bands of the Arrow Crossmen who are systematically killing the Jews of the city.

We are crossing the Chain Bridge on a dark, rainy day. As we walk across we see the statue-like figures of the German sentries, bundled up trying to keep the sharp wind blowing from the Danube. In about five minutes we reach the other shore and climbing the steep steps leading to the ornate building where the chancellery of the Apostolic Nuntio is located.

Thousands of people in our position risked their lives trying to obtain protective passports from the neutral powers who still kept their embassies open in Budapest. We thought that these passes, ornamented with impressive looking crests, would save us from being killed or deported by the Hungarian Fascists. Mother had already gone out the week before and somehow obtained the Swiss protective documents.

But rumour had it that the so called Vatican Pass was the best guaranty for the Jews you could obtain at the time in Budapest.

The lights were already on when we entered the arched gateway of the Nuntios Palace. There were only a few people around sitting in the hallway, waiting to be received on official business. After about half an hour we were invited to enter the office of a consular official. A young, owlish looking priest whom mother addressed as “Monsignore” came to receive us.

“We need this protective pass,” she told him. “Otherwise we’ll be killed or sent on a death march to Austria.”

“I know, Madame,” said the official. “But have you got the proof that you are baptized as Christians?”

Hearing this question put my mother into a very difficult position. As Jews persecuted and walking the streets without a yellow star, it would have been foolish to carry around baptismal certificates. They could easily have been found, and that would have been the end of us. On the other hand, we still lacked a set of credible false documents which would have identified us as Christians. Mother was convinced that once we had the Vatican papers we would be completely protected. Desperate that we may be sent home empty-handed my mother burst into tears.

“Monsignore, Monsignore,” she cried. “You are a Catholic priest, please have mercy on us.”

"Madame, I regret, but I am unable to do that. We have an official status as an Embassy, and this is official business."

Losing her nerves, she pulled off her wedding ring and handed it to the young priest. "Monsignore, this is the most precious thing I have. I have worn this ring since our wedding day. I am now ready to part with it as a token that I am telling you the truth that we are Christians."

I still remember the young priest shaking his head and mumbling something in embarrassment.

"Well," he said, "this is a special case, I will first have to talk to the Nuntio himself."

You can imagine how we felt while he was way consulting his superior, the papal Legate, Bishop Angelo Rotta. When he came back he had the two documents in his hands with the necessary signatures and stamps.

When we left the building we felt quite relieved. We thought that we had won and our lives would be saved. But soon our optimism had vanished. Walking down towards the Chain Bridge we heard the steps of heavy boots behind us. Looking back we saw one of the dreaded Arrow Cross men rapidly catching up with us. He wore a black uniform over his green shirt with a machine pistol slung over his shoulder. Faced with this frightful militia man, we were prepared for the worst. Yet the man was smiling. He asked us in a friendly and concerned way what we were doing near the Royal Castle at this hour so close to the curfew. Mother, who immediately recognized the dangers of this encounter said that we went to visit her mother who was dying at a nearby hospital.

"That's too bad" he said. "These are very dangerous times, there are all kinds of strange things happening in the streets. And besides," he continued. "The Russian fighter bombers may be over the city any time now. I'd better take you under my protection."

He was right. The front was about fifty kilometres south of the city and we could clearly hear the distant roar of heavy artillery during the night. Also, the Russians sent frequently over their airplanes which bombed and strafed everything that came before their sights."

"So where do you live?" he asked. "I am going to accompany you back home."

My mother, knowing that she had to keep this chivalrous man as far away as possible, said, "Oh, we live at the very outskirts of the city, please don't bother to go with us all the way there."

"But I will," he said. "It is almost curfew time and without me you wouldn't be able to cross the bridge. See those German sentries, they wouldn't let any civilians across after nine."

In a sense we were quite lucky having the Arrow Cross man as our escort because without him we would have remained stranded on the right side of the

Danube. And who would have dared to give a Jewish mother and her child shelter even in the possession of the protective documents of the Vatican? Chances were that most janitors would have handed us over to our executioners.

Having crossed the bridge our situation was becoming increasingly precarious; for we were only fifteen minutes walk from our Jewish house, and tired and hungry as we were we didn't want to roam the streets with our protector until he had smelt a rat. So my mother who had been chatting away with the militia man took another tack.

"I very much appreciate your kindness, Sir," she said. "But you should remember that like you brave fighting men, we Hungarian women have also our duties. We must take care of our homes and children and let you men go and fight the Russians and round up the deserters and other suspicious elements. Hadn't Szálasi, the Leader of our Nation, said so in one of his recent speeches? If I were you I would observe his words."

For a moment the booted warrior looked at my mother with astonishment and then said, "Well, these were the words of our Leader all right. You seem to be unlike those Jews and other riff-raff a truly patriotic Hungarian woman. OK, I let you go your way. But first leave me your address."

With the greatest relief my mother scribbled something on a piece of paper and handed it to the militia man. He raised his right arm in the Arrow Cross salute and shouted “Endurance, long live Szálasi.” He turned into one of the broad boulevards and disappeared. That was the last time that we saw him

A week later, having obtained false papers, we had left the Jewish house and had gone underground to begin a new phase of our precarious existence.

At the Salesian Brothers

To avoid being caught by the roving Arrow-Cross militia who were gunning for the Jews as well as for deserters, mother and I had decided to go underground. We had chosen this rather dangerous life-style after we saw how my aunt and her second husband had been led away from the apartment after a round up by these armed fanatics; both of them, as we soon had learnt were taken on a death march to the Austrian frontier. For the time being at least my mother and I managed to escape being caught because she was considered too old and I too young by the organizers of these "evacuations." We felt, however, that soon it would be our turn to be caught by these bandits and forced to march more than 150 miles toward Austria. The Jews who were rounded up at a time when the Soviet Army was already well inside Hungary were to be employed in the armament factories of the Third Reich. We knew that a lot of Jews had never made it to the frontier. Many were so weakened that they couldn't continue the forced march and were regularly shot by their guards and left lying on the highway where they were killed.

A day or so after we had gone underground, we saw groups of policemen together with Arrow-Cross bandits heading toward the houses where the Jews were concentrated. As the rain was coming down heavily, my mom wanted to return to our "Jewish House" to pick up an umbrella. But as soon as I saw these ominous para-military units I knew immediately that they were going to collect the rest of the remaining Jews who had temporarily been spared from the deportation order. It took me quite a while to convince my mother that the umbrella might cost our lives. We learnt later that I was right: everyone regardless of their age had been ordered out from their rooms to the street to start the foot march to Vienna. (An elderly couple I knew, a kindly physician and his wife, had killed themselves rather than to share the fate of their neighbours).

If there hadn't been Christian people who were willing to provide us with hiding places, we would probably never have survived. At first, mother and I kept together, changing quarters almost daily. Later, she was lucky enough to obtain perfect false identification papers: she now figured as a refugee woman who had been driven by the advancing Soviet Army from a provincial town. As a result, she could lead a fairly normal life which only very few Jews on the run could do. As my false ID was pretty primitive,

I would have endangered my mother if I had continued to stay with her. Thanks to the help of our Christian contacts, I landed in a children's home under the protection of both the Vatican and the Spanish government. Unfortunately, my stay there was rather short because the Arrow-Cross men, unwilling to observe diplomatic agreements, were continuously threatening to move into this nominally extra-territorial compound to haul away the children who were protected by two neutral countries. We would probably have been marched to the Danube, stripped naked and killed by submachine gun fire like so many others during that bitterly cold winter.

My mother was as surprised as she was filled with anxiety when she saw me appear so unexpectedly after I left the precarious shelter for children at the other end of the city. She had to act quite quickly for if I had stayed with her we would both have aroused the suspicion of the all powerful janitor of the building where she was staying. This woman (whom unfortunately I was to meet later) was a fervent right-wing fanatic; she was in cahoots with the Arrow-Cross men and informed them regularly about the people living in that big apartment building. It took my mother a few telephone calls to find another refuge for me. I was to go to the Salesian Brothers who cared for young apprentices and housed them in their monastery at the north-eastern outskirts of the city.

It was after a long streetcar ride well into the evening when we arrived at the Catholic institution which was to shelter me. We entered a dark building which smelled of mould and a faint whiff of incense. We were led into a big room where we were received by a roundish affable priest who assured my mother that I would be taken good care of in this home for young workers.

I was terribly sad when my mother left me, but I was careful to conceal my feelings from the priest who had taken charge of me.

In a very short time, Brother Sz. found out a great deal about me. Among other things, he learnt that I came from a well-to-do family, that my parents and I had converted to the Lutheran faith and that I loved to play the piano. He asked me to perform for him at an old out-of-tune upright, which I did. He appeared to be quite impressed and asked me to come and sit on the sofa next to him. What happened after a few minutes left me rather flabbergasted, to say the least. Drawing nearer and nearer to me, Brother Sz. pulled me into his lap started to feel me up. As a young, sexually unexperienced boy I simply didn't know what to make of his behaviour. What I felt was a kind of tickling as his fingers gradually moved up my body. What I found very strange was that he kept talking as if nothing had happened while this was going on. I, of course, didn't try to resist his advances because I knew how very much I was dependent on him. If he had touched my penis - which fortunately he never did - I would probably had become quite alarmed.

After this strange episode he handed me a Catholic Catechism. He said, "You are going to memorize a few pages of this book every day and after I have tested you, I will let you play the piano." As I was very keen to keep up my repertory, I did what he ordered me to do.

Under the wings of Brother Sz., my life became quite interesting at the Salesians. Knowing, as he did, that I was fairly good at the piano, he asked me one day to play the organ at the daily mass.

Unable to refuse him I went up to the organ loft and observed the organist who was soon to leave the city to join his relatives in western Hungary before the Russian Army had reached Budapest. It didn't take me long before I sat down and played the organ during the sacred services. It was a routine which also allowed me to improvise and try out the various registers on this old instrument which I loved to do despite the fact that I had never played the organ before. Another of my tasks was to ring with a few other boys the church bells, which was a fairly good exercise. Last but not least, I had to help preparing sour kraut putting the leaves into big barrels. It was a rather smelly and difficult job, which I hated.

When I had the time I would walk up to the attic where I could observe the flashes and listen to the distant thunder of the Russian and German artilleries which were engaged in a battle not too far from Budapest. The front was drawing ever nearer and the air raids had become increasingly frequent. I remember sitting at dinner one evening, when suddenly the building was shaken by a huge explosion. We heard later that a house received a direct hit by a Russian bomb in our immediate neighbourhood and all the people in the building were killed by the explosion.

I remember another episode which showed how insecure I was in this Catholic home for young workers.

We were already asleep when we were awakened by loud voices and heavy boot steps. A few Arrow-Crossmen entered the big hall which served as our sleeping quarters. They went to every bed and trained a flashlight on the face of each boy. Fortunately, they didn't ask for IDs. Apparently, they were trying to hunt down deserters from the Hungarian Army which was desperately trying to stop the Soviets before they reached Budapest.

A few days later I was called into the study of the Abbot. He told me that I should leave the monastery as soon as I could because he had learnt from friendly sources that the Arrow-Crossmen had smelt a rat and were preparing another, much more dangerous raid.

I had no choice but to leave. I took the streetcar back to the centre of the city and headed for the building where my mother lived.

Budapest Christmas, 1944

I cannot help remembering when the Xmas lights go on, how I spent Xmas Eve back in 1944 when I was hiding out from the Arrow Cross men in Budapest.

For weeks now I had been on the run from the Hungarian Nazis, the so called Arrow-Crossmen. Ever since they came to power in mid-October these armed bandits made it their prime objective to hunt down and kill the Jews who escaped the Auschwitz gas chambers. Since mid-November, we heard the sound of gun fire drawing nearer, hoping that we would soon be liberated. Yet despite the overwhelming power of the Soviet army, the battle dragged on and the possibility of being get caught by the roving Fascist militia was becoming ever greater. Like many Jews, I had gone underground to escape these bloody killers. I carried false documents posing as a refugee from Eastern Hungary from a town that I had never been to. While I was lucky to be sheltered by a number of Christian families, I frequently had to change my hiding places, for they could keep me only for a few days on account of suspicious neighbours and dangerous janitors, who were often the trustees of the Arrow Cross men.

Thanks to the efforts of a network of Hungarians who risked their lives to save the remaining Jews in Budapest, I had found refuge in the apartment of a music teacher shortly before Christmas. He and his family lived in a tall building on one of the great boulevards of the city. After hiding out at a rather rough and Spartan Catholic boarding school for young apprentices in one the distant suburbs, it was a terrific luxury to be sheltered in this comfortable and well appointed apartment. The first thing I saw when I came in was a wonderfully decorated tall Xmas tree. It was hung with numerous baubles and lots of colourfully wrapped scrumptious soft candies we used to call "salon sugar." At the top of the tree there was a big shining silver star illuminated by a great many candles. I was equally excited by the elegant baby grand piano which I very much hoped to play.

Even though I was very much filled with anxiety on account of my uncertain and dangerous situation I have enjoyed tremendously the company of these brave and generous people. They allowed me to spend hours at the piano and treated me as well as their two young children. Despite the severe rationing they had managed to prepare a very rich Xmas Eve dinner with a huge deliciously prepared goose with wonderfully seasoned red cabbage and dumplings.

For dessert we had a traditional Xmas sweet, freshly baked poppy seed and walnut rolls called beiglie.

We had just started on the main dish when there was a tremendous explosion and the sky lit up from the west. We first thought that it was a bomb dropped by one of the Soviet airplanes which kept raiding the city. But then in short succession there started a tremendous din coming from different directions and we soon realized that these weren't airplanes but concentrated artillery fire. The table and the chandeliers began to tremble, yet surprisingly, we kept on eating rather than moving down to the air-raid shelter. I often ask myself why we hadn't taken flight that evening leaving everything behind. The only thing that occurs to me is that we really wanted to enjoy this very special meal despite the imminent danger of being blown to pieces or buried under the ruins of the collapsing building. I tend to believe that we greatly underestimated the savage bombardment for we considered it more as a rather unpleasant spectacle than an imminent danger. It was only the next morning that we found out that the Soviet troops had closed in on Budapest and that the terrible barrage was part of the sudden, unexpected offensive.

A few days after the Russians liberated our part of the city I happened to walk past the building where I had spent Xmas Eve. When I looked up to the fourth floor to where my hosts used to live, I saw that it was partly blown away. The nice black grand piano slid down between two floors hanging vertically among the ruins of two apartments

The Test

I had very little choice but to take refuge with my mother in early January. By then I couldn't find any hiding place from the marauding Hungarian Nazis, the so called Arrow Cross men, who were massacring the Jews in Budapest. Raiding the "Jewish Houses," they marched their victims to the Danube embankments and shot them *en masse* into the frozen river.

Fortunately, my mother, who had gone also underground, was in a much better position than I was. Posing as a refugee from the advancing Soviet Army she had surprisingly little difficulty obtaining new identity papers. As a result, she was able to move into a non-Jewish house and play the rôle of a homeless Christian country woman. Making my way to the building where she was living I saw for the first time the massive walls of the Budapest ghetto where many thousands of Jews were forced to live under inhuman conditions. The house where I was heading to bordered on that sinister enclosure which was guarded day and night by trigger-happy Arrow Cross men. Because of the continuous artillery fire of the Soviet Army battling its way from the outskirts toward the centre of the city I often had to duck to avoid being wounded or killed by the exploding mortar missiles which landed at irregular intervals on the streets.

When I finally arrived I found all the people of the building in the air-raid shelter. Before meeting my mother I ran into a good friend of the family, a Christian woman, who was very much aware of my condition. She told me what the new name of my mother was and suggested that I should call her as auntie Zsóka. I was also advised that I should pose as a close acquaintance of her from the same city from where she was supposed to have fled from the Russians.

What I got myself into was not only an unusual but also very dangerous situation for both mother and myself. How to communicate with "auntie Zsóka" before we spontaneously reverted to the mother-son relationship? And how long would it be before people in this overcrowded place would overhear this fatal slip and as a result might soon find out who we really were? I am still very much surprised that we had managed to wear these masks to the very end while we were able to discuss matters concerning our hazardous situation. If this weren't enough a few days after my arrival I suddenly recognized one of my classmate among the many people in the shelter and I am pretty sure that he had also recognized me. But then something happened that I had never expected. We looked at each other, but then we both turned away as if we were strangers. (I suspect that knowing how very close the Russians were, he had the good sense not to betray me. Life underground had its ironic moments. As mother had saved many of our fine cigarettes she encouraged me to barter them for alcoholic drinks. I had become so adept at these transactions that one day I was called a Jew by one of my customers.

There were also gruesome moments. One day in a pause from the continuous air-raids of the low - flying Soviet fighter bombers, I went up to the courtyard and saw a simple wooden coffin there. As it wasn't sealed I lifted its cover. What I saw was the open and bloody skull of a woman with parts of her brain covering her face. When I asked how she had died, I was told that she had shot herself because she was cheated by one of the Hungarian soldiers billeted in our building with whom she was desperately in love.

There was a considerable increase in the bombing and artillery salvos hitting our street as the Russians got nearer and as a result we could hardly leave our shelter to get some fresh air. But there were also times when suddenly the terrible din had unexpectedly stopped. I remember one evening standing in the courtyard enjoying the pleasant silence. Then suddenly from very far I heard the sound of a gun or a mortar being fired. Immediately thereafter I heard the eerie whistle of the shell which seemed to have taken ages to travel through its trajectory until it exploded a great distance away. I found this aural spectacle so fascinating that I keenly waited for its repetition, but in vain. Not long afterwards, the artillery salvos started again and I couldn't but leave in a hurry down to the air-raid shelter.

A few days later something happened that I feared would really endanger my life. We all knew about the woman janitor of the building who was a rabid Nazi. We were told that she had fled the city. But now the news had come that she was back in the house, wounded with a bullet in her arm which hit her while she was trying to reach the German lines. My only hope was that the Russians would reach our street before she was fit enough to start her hunt for deserters and hidden Jews.

A day or so later the lights went on in the cubicle reserved for this much feared woman. With a bandage around her arm she was studying the list of people who had sought shelter in the house. One by one she called out the names of those whose identity she found suspect. When my turn had come I had to show her my identity card (which, incidentally, was not a forgery but was seemingly obtained by legal means by a clever lawyer. What counted was that it was the ID of an "Aryan" boy of my age whom I had to impersonate while I was in hiding).

"So you are István Kovács," she said. "How did you get here?"

To answer her question I had to repeat the scenario which was invented by the lawyer. I told her, as instructed, that I was also one of the refugees from Eastern Hungary and found through an acquaintance my way to the house. But that wasn't enough for her because obviously she suspected me to be a Jew. I of course, denied quite vehemently that I was one of those she had been after.

"I am not a Jew, I am a Lutheran. I have been a student at a Lutheran lycée for the last two years," I said.

"Well then prove it to me," she commanded. I couldn't do better than to recite the Lord's Prayer, certain passages from the Bible and also sing a few chorals to her.

"Well, you might have been a good student memorizing all this stuff, but that does not prove that you aren't a Jew," she insisted. "There is only one way to prove your identity is to see whether you are circumcised or not. I am going to get a doctor who will be able to determine whether you are lying or not," she said.

I was terribly frightened when the doctor appeared and led me to the toilet. When I dropped my trousers he inspected my penis for a long time without saying anything to me. When we returned, he gave the woman an ambivalent report. He couldn't quite determine whether I was circumcised, he said. But that was not enough for her.

"In that case the boy will be sent to the Arrow-Cross centre where a commission would soon find out whether he is a Jew or not," she said.

Even though the battle had become so fierce that there was no way of sending me over to the headquarters of the expert Jew-hunters, I felt pretty sure that they were going to catch me. When I told my mother what happened, she said, "If they send you over, I will join you and we will both die together."

We waited all night and part of the next day for the black uniformed killers. But instead of them, those who came were fortunately the first Soviet soldiers who entered the air-raid shelter.

Budapest, March 1945

Having spent almost over a year away from our apartment, mother and I decided to walk over to the other end of the city to see what had happened to it in our absence. It was in May, 1944 that we had to pack our things and move into one of the so called "Jewish Houses" following the orders of the Hungarian Fascist authorities. That's where we used to live before we had gone underground to escape the marauding Arrow Cross bands who had nothing better to do than to capture the Jews and kill them. To save our effects in our apartment, we invited a Christian woman, Mrs Z, to move in to our place hoping that she would take good care of the many things that we had to leave behind. An acquaintance of one of my father's friends, she was a youngish, divorced woman who moved in with her teenage daughter a month after the Germans occupied Hungary. As she was an amateur poet and obviously quite proud of her talents, we had to sit and listen to her recitations for hours on end. Before we left for the "Jewish House," she gave us her word that she was going to take good care of our effects.

As the Germans blew up all the bridges of the Danube during the siege of Budapest, we had to cross over a fairly primitive and narrow pontoon bridge to reach the other shore to make our way to our apartment. Once we got over, we had to find a route through endless stretches of ruined streets. This was the part of the city where the Germans engaged in the fiercest resistance to save "Fortress Budapest" from the Red Army. Everywhere we went we felt the nauseating stench of death mixed with the bitter odour of burnt out cars and tanks. On our way we saw an odd sight, the front part of a light German glider buried into the roof of a tall building with the rear end of its fuselage sticking out over the ruined remnants of that once fashionable dwelling. I thought that the plane must have been on its way to a nearby makeshift airport when it rammed into the roof, or was shot down.

It was a very long walk considering our tortuous progress through the ruined streets. Gradually, the bombed out or half destroyed buildings became rarer, which gave us some hope that our house would still stand. And so it did, though it was rather pockmarked by numerous hits, the traces of the German's desperate but foiled breakout from the encircled city.

When we rang the bell of our apartment, Mrs Z opened the door. I will never forget the surprise on her face when she recognized us. "Are you still alive?" she cried. Apart from a few bullet holes and broken windows, the apartment seemed to be in relatively good order. After telling her how we had managed to survive mother asked, "Were you able to preserve our things that we left behind?"

"Oh, God no!" Mrs Z answered. "These damned Russians broke into the apartment and robbed everything they could. They took away even my underwear. But at least they didn't rape me like they have Miss B the spinster daughter of the old upholsterer."

Just before we were to leave my mother went up to one of the closets and opened it. "And what are these?" she asked, pointing at her dresses and costumes which supposedly were cleaned out by the marauding Russian soldiers. She also found a number of suits from my father as well as perfumes and various toilet articles.

Soon after our visit we moved back to our apartment, but by then Mrs Z was no longer there. But she didn't disappear altogether. A short while later we learned that she denounced my mother with the help of her lover, an ex- Fascist police officer, for having blackmailed her - a charge that was as untrue as it was ridiculous. As mother and I were keen to emigrate to the US she had to have a clear judicial record before we were to be granted a visa. After learning about the circumstances of these accusations the police immediately dropped these absurd and malicious charges.

A Hanging

Budapest, February 1945. There is a big crowd gathering in one of the principal squares of the city. The Germans are still fighting on the other side of the river and their shells still land on our side liberated by the Soviet Army. But few people seem to care about the possibility of being hit or killed by the exploding mortars because they are all excited to see the execution of two army sergeants who tormented and killed scores of Hungarian Jewish Slav workers in Russia.

We don't have to wait too long for the arrival of the car which carries the two condemned. The public prosecutor reads out the death sentence, the priest performs the last rites and now the final act begins. As there are no gallows two lamp-posts will do. The first condemned is lifted onto a table requisitioned from a neighbouring cafe. In a minute he is swinging in the air, but suddenly the rope breaks and he is lying on the ground. But he is hoisted up again and now he is safely on his way to eternity. As the other condemned is further away I can,t see quite clearly what is going on. But this time the hangman must have learnt his lesson because the condemned remains hanging at the end of the rope.

For the crowd this is more than a spectacle: it is an occasion to express its immense hatred against those horrible, bloodthirsty soldiers, gendarmes, and roving Arrow Cross murderers who slaughtered thousands of innocent people during the Second World War. The fury of the crowd has no limit. They shout, they curse, and some people in tears are speaking about the horrible slaughters which took place in the city during the last two months. Suddenly the crowd breaks through the thin cordon of the policemen. They run up to the two dead soldiers, hit the corpses and cover their faces with spittle. I notice a young man with a stick hurrying towards one of the condemned. He is aiming his stick quite carefully and with a sudden movement he thrusts it in the eye of one of one of the dead soldiers. This last scene I will never forget.

Part 2

Escape from Hungary

At "Gaudiopolis," the Children's Republic.

One day, seven months after the Soviet Army occupied Budapest, mother took me to the Buda Hills. It was a beautiful September day as we walked up the steep, narrow road near the western outskirts of the city. When we finally reached our destination, a big white villa, my mother said, "I am sure you would be much better off here than living with me in our apartment."

As a widow, my mother was dirt-poor and had hardly anything to eat, like so many others in most of the cities and towns of Hungary at the time. A couple of months after the siege of Budapest, she had sent me to the countryside in a feed-the-children programme. When I came back, she was still unable to keep me, so at the advice of another widow, she was now taking me to a special institution that cared for orphaned children.

One of the first persons we talked to was a very good looking, aristocratic woman, who after a friendly exchange with my mother, put me in a wooden tub and gave me a good wash. I loved the smell of the rough laundry soap and the feel of the tub because it brought back one of my very first memories, another bath given by a nanny at our vacation home east of Budapest. After my mother left, I was taken to a big room, with quite a few rows of two-tiered beds which was the sleeping quarter of the older boys. I was in the company of orphaned kids who, like me, had nowhere else to go. Even though I was afraid that I would have problems getting used to life in the children's home, I had surprisingly little difficulty getting adjusted to it. Despite the varied backgrounds of the boys, some of whose parents were closely associated with deeply conservative, if not Fascist circles, I had hardly any trouble getting along with them. There was a remarkable *esprit de corps* among the boys which I had noticed pretty soon. This sense of community came from a remarkable man, the head of the children's colony, the Lutheran pastor, Gábor Sztehlo.

As far as Protestant clergymen are concerned, the "Sir Reverend" ("Nagytiszteletes Úr") as we called him, was quite an uncommon figure. With the help of the Swiss Red Cross he founded thirty-two children's homes during the war and saved over a thousand Jewish children from the raging Arrow Cross bands. An episode from the time when the Soviet Army occupied Budapest shows in a telling way, his unusually brave and self-sacrificing character. When some Soviet soldiers seized one of the boys that he had protected - a boy who happened to have blond hair - the Russians had mistaken him for a hidden German soldier and were ready to execute him. Realising what was going to happen, Sztehlo threw himself before the youngster in his clerical garb saying, "If you shoot him you will have to shoot me, too."

Nonplussed by this unusual gesture, the soldiers lowered their rifles and let the boy go. But what really distinguished the Protestant pastor was his readiness to save and care for everyone, regardless of their religion. What's more, unlike so many other missionary-minded clergymen, he never forced anyone to become a Lutheran. It was his exceptional character, radiating love and a powerful sense of community, that had a profound influence on us living in the children's home that he had founded and directed.

What made my stay in this refuge particularly valuable was that I was living in a children's republic. Called "Gaudiopolis - The City of Love" - it had its own government with its ministers, law courts and economic and cultural institutions, all run by us but also in conjunction with Sztehlo himself. His rôle was entirely non-authoritarian and as a result, his advice and suggestions were readily accepted.

I really thrived in this unusual environment. For the first time in my life I had discovered my abilities and could make good use of them. Without needing the urgings of my mother or certain teachers, I spontaneously engaged in activities that contributed to the life of the community. I wrote, for instance, articles for the wall newspaper and played the piano at the Reverend's divine services. I had also done a number of chores and learnt skills, which I had never dreamed to have been able to do. But my mother, too, had profited from my stay at "Gaudiopolis." As an excellent pianist, she regularly visited the Children's Republic to give piano lessons to the kids, in exchange for which she received much needed food from the stocks of the institution.

I have always known how much I had gained from my stay in this children's village, especially during my first difficult period as an immigrant in Canada. A few years ago, I was fortunate enough to find the Sztehlo foundation on the internet which enabled me to get in touch with one of the fellow "Sztehlo children." I had learnt from him that a number of former citizens of

Gaudiopolis would be present at the annual wreath laying ceremony. I promptly made up my mind to travel to Budapest and be present at the annexe of a Lutheran church up in the Castle district where the commemoration was to take place.

I still remember how excited I was on my way to that old church whose services I had regularly attended when in the early 1940s, I was a student at the Lutheran lycée in Budapest. Would I recognize any of the "Sztehlo children" and would they recognize me after sixty years or so? I asked myself. And what would we have to say to each other? When I entered the room where everyone for the memorial meeting had gathered, I could identify only a few of the persons who were present as those I had known at the children's republic. When I talked to them they seemed to be somewhat reluctant to revive some of our common memories. And there were others to whom I had to introduce myself to learn who they were. I remembered their names alright but the faces had changed quite profoundly since I had seen them the last time. I recall meeting an old gentleman who, after introducing himself, said that he was E. Sch. He was one of the boys I was particularly fond of while I was living at Gaudiopolis. Unfortunately, like some of the 'old boys,' he wasn't very forthcoming. Perhaps this was due to the relatively brief meeting which, after the wreath laying ceremony was largely devoted to official business. I suspect, however, that I too was somewhat unrecognizable to the others. Perhaps my changed physique and my rusty Hungarian might have given them the impression of a "foreigner."

I could have phoned E. Sch, but I was in two minds about getting in touch with him. Unfortunately, I will never be able to do so because I have learnt a short time ago by a chain-email from the convener of the "Sztehlo children" that E. Sch had passed away after a short illness.

My Escape Attempt

In the spring of 1949 I had no other wish but to escape from Hungary. This was the year the Communists manoeuvred themselves into key positions of the government and were beginning to use their famed "salami technique." They were gradually slicing away the power from the remaining political parties until they got total control of the whole country. This was also the time of some of the great political show trials as well as the beginning of a wave of arrests by the security police, the dreaded AVO. As someone of bourgeois origins I had no chance to become a university student despite my high marks at the Lycée. If I had remained in the country I had no choice but become a factory or a construction worker. This would be the only way to show my allegiance to the "Worker's Republic," as I was told by a distant relative who occupied a very high position in the Communist Party. Opportunists as they were, some of my fellow students knew how to endear themselves to the authorities. These boys who came from similar bourgeois backgrounds as I, became agitators in the Communist youth organizations adhering to the party-line right down to the letter. I was very suspicious of these turncoats because they had the habit of spying on their teachers. I wouldn't have been surprised if they had reported me if I had said things which sounded reactionary to these opportunistic converts of the political order.

But how to escape from a country that surrounded itself with endless barbed wire entanglements, mine-fields and other ingenious traps guarded by specially trained border guards? Still, there were some people who managed to make their way over to Austria, but their numbers were rapidly decreasing day by day. Most of those trying to leave the country illegally 56were caught, often beaten up and automatically sentenced to stiff terms in prisons or labour camps. Under the circumstances my wish to escape from Hungary appeared to be pretty hopeless. And yet, I came up with an escape plan that may just have worked. I thought that I could use a visit to the grave of my father who was shot by the Nazis very near the Austrian border as an alibi for getting close to the frontier area. Knowing, as I did, that the secret police was controlling all the trains and cars leaving in the direction of the border I had a document justifying my presence in the western edge of Hungary. It was a clipping from a newspaper which described how he was caught after his escape attempt from a forced labour camp and how he was beaten and killed by an SS sergeant just a few weeks before the Russians liberated the area. Before I left Budapest I had spoken to one of the fellow prisoners of my father. Apart from finding out more about the last days of my father, I also wanted to get more information about the lay of the land from where I would attempt to escape to Austria. I learnt from him that where my father was buried was at the edge of a tiny village. His grave was not far from the big swampy region of the Neusiedler Lake, part of which belonged to Austria. I knew full well how dangerous my plan was, but I was so obsessed with escaping from the country that I considered my foolhardy attempt as a calculated risk. If I hadn't shown a lot of self-confidence for my escape plan I doubt whether my mother would have permitted me to leave for this adventure.

It was on a bright April morning when I boarded the express train in the direction of Csoma from where I was to take a local train to the village of Acsalag where my father was buried. To my surprise, I didn't meet any security men on the express, but I was almost certain that they would stop me during the last stage of my journey.

While I was waiting to change the train, a rather robust-looking old peasant came up to me. “Where are you from?” he asked. “And what are you doing here?” he continued. I gave him the news clipping and told him that I am going to visit the grave of my father. It turned out that he was the Party secretary of the region, a man who would certainly have handed me over to the secret police if I had no good way to explain why I was travelling in this closely controlled area.

When I eventually got to A, I came as the orphaned son of a Jewish forced labourer who was anxious to see the spot where his father was buried. As the killing occurred four years before some of the villagers still remembered the killing of my father. One of them told me to see the local forester because this man was present when the murder had occurred. As he was not living too far away I went straightaway to see him hoping that he would lead me to the grave of my father.

I found the forester both kind and very helpful. He led me to a meadow at a clearing of a large forest where my father used to cut down trees with his comrades. They were working in the area to supply materials for the so called South Wall, a fortified defence ring which was supposed to stop the Soviet Army on its advance to Vienna.

He pointed to the foot of a hillock and said, "That's where your father is buried." It was one of those countless unmarked graves that dotted that border area.

I was surprised that he knew the exact spot, but I thought that as a forester he had a very good sense of the terrain and therefore he knew how to pinpoint the plot where my father's remains rested. He said that he was present at the burial and he remembered well that while the grave of my father was dug by other forced labourers, the SS killer warned them that if they made the grave any wider he would shoot them next to my father. After we viewed the spot where my father was buried, he invited me to his house for a glass of wine. I thought that the time had come to reveal to him the real purpose of my visit. When I told him that I actually wanted to slip across the border he didn't appear to be too surprised. What's more, he also gave me directions for a path which would lead to Austria. Before I left him he went to his desk and came back with a small, oblong, yellowish object. “I kept the bullet that killed your father,” he said. He handed it to me and said, “Here it is, take it with you.”

The same evening, after dark, I started to make my way toward the Austrian border. I soon found myself in a swampy region and I noticed that the path I was supposed to take was getting wetter and wetter. After half an hour or so, I was walking in ever-rising water. I was getting pretty disoriented as well as sickened by the sulphurous stench of the swampy water. I have no idea how long I had kept walking, but after a while I felt that if I continued on like that, I might get irretrievably lost in this treacherous terrain, or even worse, I may sink down and perish in the quagmire. So I turned back and retraced my way to the distant village. I arrived well after midnight, completely soaked and muddy. When the woman who put me up asked what happened I said that I had taken a walk along the swamp and I had lost my bearings in the total darkness. I very much doubt whether she believed what I told her. Fortunately, she did not question me further and even helped to dry my wet clothing.

The next morning, which happened to be Easter Sunday, I caught the express train back to Budapest. When my mother saw me entering our apartment she embraced me but drew immediately back when she smelled the sulphurous stench of my mud-caked suit.

For a while I carried the bullet which killed my father around with me. But one very rainy evening I took it from my pocket and threw it into the gutter.

Escape from Hungary

It's shortly after two in the afternoon. It's January 25, 1950. I hastily kiss my mother knowing that in about half an hour I have to be at our meeting place at the Southern Railway Station of Budapest where I am to meet the guide who is going to take me across the frontier. The man who was going to smuggle me and my companions out of the country was sent over from Austria by my aunt and her husband who had managed to flee the country half a year earlier.

The price for this dangerous trip was very stiff. But my mother who had let me go on my failed escape attempt nine months earlier wanted to make sure that I would now be in safe hands during this very risky track across the border. So he gave the guide practically all her saved dollars which was quite a considerable sum at the time in Hungary.

Before I left I knew that my cousin will be with me, but had no idea that ten other people would join us at the railway station. Most of us took our seats in different compartments fearing that if we were congregated together the secret policemen making their rounds in the train might get wind of our intentions even though we all had our alibis. We were to leave the train at a town still fairly far away from the frontier station to avoid the suspicion of the border officials. We were told that we had to walk twenty miles or so until we reached the fortified border area which we didn't take too seriously before we boarded the train. What we were really afraid of was that we might get caught by the secret policemen even before we started on our perilous walk towards the border.

It was a beautiful winter afternoon when we left Budapest. As the train picked up speed the windows began to be covered by sheets of ice which gave us an idea how very cold it must have been outside. But the cold was not our immediate concern because we were thinking of all those people who had been caught while attempting to cross the border. They were usually badly beaten up before sentenced and sent away for years into prisons or even worse into prison camps. My uncle and aunt before they had escaped provided themselves with poison pills to escape the fate of those who fell into the hands of the secret police. I have no doubt that they would have killed themselves, because five years earlier they both experienced the horrors of a death march organized by the Nazis towards the end of the war.

I don't know why but on this particular afternoon no one came into our compartment to ask for our identity cards and inquire about the reason for our trip which was to take us so close to the frontier. I guess that our guide, who had done this trip a good many times before, knew what train to take to avoid the roving policemen.

It was already dark when we left the train and that's when we began to feel how very cold it was. We walked for half an hour or so to reach the house at the outskirts of the town where we were to have dinner and have a couple of hours of rest before we set out on our march to the frontier. It was in this rather simple home of a peasant couple who undoubtedly got a fair bit of money for feeding us and putting us up for a few hours. That's where I got acquainted with members of our group. They were mostly middle-class people, much older than my cousin and I who were ready to be led by our guide across the border. The man who was to lead us to freedom was quite an adventurous character. He used to be a soldier in an engineering unit of the Hungarian army and as such he knew his way with the land mines which were planted along the Hungarian frontier. After the war he joined the French Foreign Legion, but after a few years he had deserted that formidable and notorious military organization and made his home in Salzburg, Austria. Rather than leaving the country for overseas like so many refugees, he thought that he could make an excellent living by applying his skills as a sapper and as a soldier. Knowing, as he did, that many people from Hungary would pay a fortune to escape to the west, he became what was called at the time a "professional man smuggler." With good contacts in the Hungarian emigrant community he was given the addresses of those who could pay for his specialized services in the old country. As far as I know he had made at least half a dozen trips to get his customers across the border. He didn't think of saving money however much he earned and as a result he was forced into his perilous way of life which he appeared to have enjoyed. In tune with his life-style he had taken along two persons from whom he didn't demand any money: the one was his latest girl friend, the other a working class boy who had to carry tons of disks of Hungarian gypsy music in a knapsack from Budapest to Salzburg, Austria.

We set out close to midnight walking for a while along a country road. Not far ahead of us were a number of locals probably returning home from an inn. I suddenly heard one of them cry "Ah, the frontier is swarming again with people". When I heard this I became quite frightened because I believed that they might report us to the next patrol. However, I believe now that they may have looked at us in amusement rather than enmity having seen similar groups making their way up toward the frontier.

After a while, we left the country road and began to make our way across the fields. Trekking across the frozen and rough terrain became increasingly difficult. After a couple of hours, the older people became increasingly fatigued and they had to be continuously urged on. I noticed that after a while they began to drop their bags and briefcases despite the fact that they must have contained changes of cloth and important documents.

It was still dark when we arrived to the frontier area. The first things that we saw were the watchtowers which our guide had carefully avoided. Then we came to a patch of land where he made us stop. He crept forward with some kind of an instrument and stopped from time to time. All I saw was that he was touching the ground and digging at something. He was actually tracing and defusing the land mines. After a good quarter of an hour he motioned us to follow him in a single file. Soon we arrived at the barbed wire which barred our way to the no man's land. He took a huge wire cutter from his knapsack and cut through the entanglements. For some reason, he did not leave much room to slip through the wire. As carefully as I tried to get across I tore a huge hole in my trousers, but fortunately without hurting my leg. Pointing to a small river our guide said, "That's already in Nickelsdorf, Austria."

Even though we had luckily reached the other side of the border we weren't safe yet for we were still in the Soviet Zone of Austria. We had to reach Vienna to get into one of the western zones of that divided city. The only way to get there was to take the early worker's train to the capital. As we couldn't stop at the railway station of this small village for fear of being picked up by the border patrols of the Soviet Army we had to jump unto the slowly moving train. The closer the train moved toward me the more frightened I got but I somehow still managed to get on the stairs where I was grabbed by the guide. I learnt later that some of the older people couldn't get on the train but somehow they had managed to make their way to Vienna.

Terribly fatigued and with badly frozen toes I arrived an hour later to the East Station of Vienna. The first things we saw after we left the train were huge posters with Stalin, Lenin and Marx at a square adjoining the station.

If that weren't enough, loudspeakers blared the patriotic marches and songs of the Soviet Union. I suddenly felt trapped. But our guide said, just walk through the street and we will be soon in the American zone. And so we arrived in a peaceful still quiet quarter of the city pockmarked by half-ruined buildings. After a hot breakfast we arrived to our temporary quarters. We got into a small apartment which didn't contain enough sleeping facilities. So I slipped with my cousin into the same bed and fell promptly asleep. It was quite dark when I woke up again. It was around eight in the evening. I think that I must have slept about ten hours.

The Friendly Gestapo Man

Hearing from an acquaintance that the International Refugee Organization (IRO) was looking for clerks who were bilingual in English and German. I applied for the job and was promptly hired. That's how I managed to move out from the Jewish Displaced Persons Camp where I felt too much constrained. This enabled me to move to Enns, a small town in Upper Austria from where I could commute to another DP camp where the offices of the IRO were located.

Enns at the time of the Cold War was quite well known because it was one of the principal checkpoints between the American and Russian zones of divided Austria. Returning from work I used to look down from the town toward the railway line which crossed the smallish Enns river. From there I could watch the trains stopping at either side of the river. Seeing the Russian and American MPs boarding the wagons to check the IDs of the passengers I couldn't but remember my escape from Hungary earlier in the winter.

One day a postcard from one of my mother's Hungarian friends arrived. It said that a man smuggling people out of Hungary was sent for her and that she had already managed to get across the border. Knowing that she would be heading for Salzburg where her sister Anikó and her brother-in-law lived, I took the next train to Mozart's city to meet my mother.

I would have loved to stay with her, but that was, at the time impossible because, unwilling to move to a Displaced Persons Camp she had to find a job as soon as possible. There was yet another reason why she had to look after herself. Her sister and her brother-in-law who lived in a comfortable hotel wouldn't take her in despite the fact that they had lots of money. In fact, my aunt was so stingy that she made my mom pay back later the packed lunch Anikó gave me when I had left Salzburg for the Jewish DP Camp at Steyr. As long as she lived, my mother had kept the itemized account for the fruit and sandwiches among her papers.

My mother became a maid of all works at the home of an American master sergeant. She not only had to cook for the family but she also did the laundry and cared for the two children. What's more, as a pianist, she also gave piano lessons to the older boy. I used to visit her on my trips to Salzburg and was surprised how well she adjusted to this very demanding job.

Learning about the difficult situation of my mother, my father's cousin as well as her own cousin, who both lived in London, had sent her a monthly allowance that allowed her to quit her job. This enabled her to look for a room where she could live until she had received her immigration visa from America. I too, was in the fortunate position of having a job with another refugee organisation in Salzburg, which gave me a chance to stay with my mother.

It didn't take us long to get suitable quarters. We moved to Grödig, a small village at the outskirts of the city which lay at the foot of the Untersberg. This was the tall, very picturesque mountain which according to legend held the remnants of the famous Emperor Barbarossa. As I had never lived in such a picturesque and beautiful region, I greatly enjoyed the very special atmosphere of this Alpine village.

Not long after our arrival my mother got acquainted with the woman who owned the local grocery store. Telling her about her life in Hungary, she mentioned that she was a pianist which gave the woman an idea. Wouldn't she give piano lessons to her step daughter? Mother was quite glad to accept the offer because she felt quite lonely at the village while I was away working during the day at the refugee organization.

She and her family lived in a big house over the store which was just a short distance from where we stayed. I liked to visit the family, especially because of H. the daughter with whom I got along famously. Her father, Herr F felt greatly relieved that she had me as her friend. Knowing that I came from a good family he willingly entrusted me with her daughter. As he told me, he was glad of having me as the boyfriend of her daughter because he was very much afraid that she might get involved with the lusty village boys.

He had shown his sympathy for me in a number of ways. Once before I took H to Salzburg, he went down to the store and gave us a big bar of Swiss milk chocolate. He also used to invite mother and me for dinner washed down with plenty of booze. Last but not least he taught me how to ride a bicycle which was not an easy task because I was exceptionally awkward as a young boy.

There was one thing that overshadowed my relationship with this kind and jovial man: He used to be a member of the Gestapo. He got this position as an ethnic German from Russia who left the country when the Wehrmacht had occupied Odessa. He moved to Salzburg, and because of his skills as a Russian speaker, he was employed by the Gestapo as an interpreter. He told me that he was a *"Sonderführer"* the equivalent of a technical officer. I had avoided asking him what his duties where because I dreaded finding out about the rough details of his business. As you can imagine I had rather ambivalent feelings in his company. On the one hand, I greatly enjoyed his presence. On the other , I couldn't help thinking of my father who was killed as a Jew by an SS man, quite apart from my life as a young boy who was almost caught and shot by the Fascist Arrow Cross men. What could I have done under the circumstances? Should I have told him that I was a Hungarian Jew? Knowing that he was an anti-Semite and that he had a circle of rabidly anti-Semitic friends my admission would certainly had caused a scandal. What's more I didn't want to hurt the feeling of a man who treated me so very well.

Even though I made as much as I could of this strange relationship, I felt relieved when my "friendship" came to an end with him when I left as an immigrant for Canada.

At the Displaced Persons' Camp (February, 1950)

I took the train from Salzburg to Linz on a freezing February afternoon on my way to a Jewish Displaced Person's Camp. That's where I was sent by my aunt Anikó and her second husband S. three weeks after my escape from Communist Hungary. I was somewhat apprehensive about this journey because I didn't quite know what such a refugee camp was like, even though I was assured by my relatives that I would be very well off there. When I arrived in Linz near sunset I had to change to a bus which would take me to Steyr, where the DP camp was located. It was well past dinner time when I entered the administration building not far off the centre of a collection of longish wooden huts which looked very much like Wehrmacht army barracks. Through a long corridor I reached the office of the so called *"Lagerälterste"* who was the chief administrator of the camp. He was a youngish, rather impersonal Hungarian, who, after I gave him my documents from the Jewish refugee organization, handed me some bedding and assigned me to another dull, gray building where the single men were housed.

There were about two dozen people in the room which consisted of a large table and a number of two-tier bunks. Most of them spoke a funny kind of language which sounded like twisted German. Even though I could get the drift of what they said I could only answer them in German. *"Wuz bist Du Kein Yid?"* "Hey, aren't you a Jew?" one of them asked me in obvious disappointment when I answered him in German. (As I found out very soon, they were speaking Yiddish, the lingua-franca of East European Jews). There was a Hungarian Jew, a brawny young man, who seemed to have taken an immediate dislike to me. He said that I was a sissy and that he is going to show me what life in a camp was like. He was an obvious bully who would torment me until the lights had gone out.

Life was interesting in the camp but I didn't like it. As a Jewish boy from an upper-middle class background who was taught to look down on Ashkenazi Jews from the East, I had suddenly found myself thrown into their midst and had to learn to live with them. The distrust was certainly mutual. I had the impression that they sensed that I have come from a different "tribe" and as a result, many of them were quite suspicious of me. I, on the other hand, couldn't help but feel my prejudices confirmed by their distanced behaviour. I think that the main barrier between us was the language. Unable to speak Yiddish, I had to communicate in German with them, something they disliked. Understandably, this was the language of the executioners and they must have felt very uneasy hearing that tongue spoken by other Jews.

Even though I was unable to speak Yiddish, I could understand a great deal of what they were saying. I was particularly interested in the exploits of a group of young men with whom I shared a room in the camp. It appeared that they were engaged in all kind of shady transactions and as a result they made a lot of dough on the black market. What intrigued me even more were their exploits with Austrian women. In fact, I was told that it was quite easy to buy the favours of these *"Fräuleins"* and the thought that I may also sleep with some of them excited me no end. One day I accompanied one of the men to the pick-up joint in town, hoping to make some contacts with these loose girls. I must have come at the wrong time because I was sorely disappointed. Instead of the girls and women in bloom, I saw mostly rather worn, middle-aged professionals. Another thing that excited my imagination was the private life of one of my fellow countryman. He was a well-known tailor in Budapest, who must have come out with a lot of dough that he spent quite liberally on his live-in mistress. We all heard that Mr X, a man in his early fifties, was impotent and that he had to be specially stimulated by his Austrian mistress to function again as a man. He seemed to have taken a liking to me because he had taken me out a few times to various restaurants. While I didn't particularly enjoy his company, I greatly enjoyed the rich Austrian country-fare served in these establishments. One evening I found him in the company of his buddies with whom he used to discuss sex. We were about to leave to head back to the camp when he noticed me.

He said with a broad smile, "Shall we take the kid to the whorehouse?"

As I had never been in such a place I accepted his offer with obvious excitement.

When I lived in the DP camp in the winter of 1950, Steyr in upper Austria was still largely an ancient city. Along the river shore there were rows of houses which appeared as if they were built in the 17th century. And there was also an ancient wall which in part surrounded the city. When we set out for our visit to the whorehouse with Mr X and his friends, we first had to cross an old gateway and then walk for another ten minutes before we saw an isolated old building lit by a red lantern. I must say, that even while I looked forward to the visit I felt somewhat apprehensive. For I remembered my mother's warning immediately prior to my first, escape attempt. "Keep away from bad women," she said, without giving me any details.

I also remembered the stories that I had heard about gonorrhoea and in particularly about the famous "hockey-stick" treatment which involved poking with a kind of tiny disinfected brush into your urethra. And then those photos I saw in a medical book showing men whose nose was eaten away by virulent skin diseases during the last phases of syphilis. Regardless of these fears I didn't want to appear as a sissy and therefore I decided to keep my sangfroid during the adventure.

The door was opened by an oldish uniformed man who looked like a cross between a taxi-chauffeur and an army sergeant. He invited us into a rickety parlour lit by the reddish glare of a chandelier. There were a few customers there in the company of a few women. I have completely forgotten the faces of the people in that reception room, except for an immensely fat, middle-aged whore who was rubbing herself against a uniformed bus conductor. She was dressed all in green like a Tyrolean country girl. How was this thin little man, I thought, going to find his way into this towering mass of fat? But judging by the tone of the conversation of that heavy woman and her customer, I thought that they had probably been through that challenging exercise before.

After a few drinks, Mr X turned to me. "You know what, I am going to pay you for a go with a woman. And I know exactly the one who would be right for you," he said.

And then he walked up to an old stern-looking woman - the so called *Puffmutter* who ran the establishment.

"Is Clara around tonight?" he asked. "Let's get her for this young man."

The *Puffmutter* mounted the stairs and soon came back with a small woman of uncertain age, wearing nothing except thin, see-through panties and a brassier. I noticed that she had long, flowing black hair.

"Well, there is your young man Clara," Mr X said. "You know how to treat him eh?" Even though I wasn't a virgin my heart was beating real hard when I followed her up the stairs. After we got to the first floor the woman opened the door to a surprisingly large, makeshift room. There was a large commode in the corner and a smallish plastic table with a lot of knick-knacks. A pitcher and a washbowl not far from the bed obviously served the hygienic needs of her clients. I was hardly afraid of "Clara" because she handled me in quite a gentle, if not in a motherly way. I had the impression that Mr X suggested to her that she should treat me as a virgin. Everything went much slower than I had expected. I felt quite happy that she didn't make any hints that she was going to initiate someone who had not slept with a woman before. In fact, I had already known some of the "secrets" of sex because a year or so before I got the domestic servant of my cousin's grandma into bed. In the families where I came from it was not unusual to employ a pretty domestic who, it was expected, would provide the "young gentleman" with his first sexual experience. But there was another solution for the erotic enlightenment for boys of my social milieu - a visit to the brothel. My mother remembered that her father in-law told her that he would take me to an excellent bordello once I had reached the age to become sexually educated.

Shortly after I had come, thanks to the special skills of the woman, I suddenly became aware of a noise from behind a black curtain from the other end of the room. I was certain that it originated from Mr X who must have spied on me as a way to arouse himself - probably for an extra fee. When we left the brothel he asked me, "Well, did you enjoy fucking that woman?" Knowing that he probably saw everything from his hiding place, I simply said that she was OK.

In fact, I was quite angry at him for I felt that I had been utilized to help to an erection an impotent man.

Some Pictures over the Years

My maternal Grandfather, Josef Berman, Colonel doctor in the Austro-Hungarian Army

My father, Mother and I before our holiday residence

My mother's family, including her brother and sister

My two grandmothers. The one in the wheelchair is my father's mother.
The other is my mother's mother.
The picture was taken one summer near Lake Balaton.

My mother and I

My mother in regal pose

Erwin with toy automobile

A young Erwin at various ages

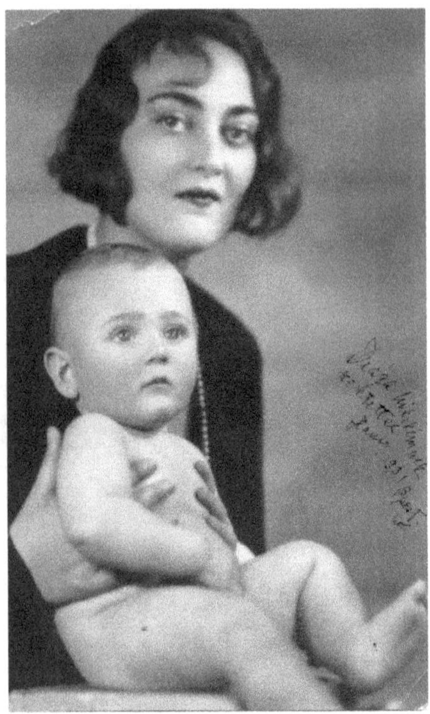

My mother with baby Erwin

My mother as a young woman on the beach of Lake Balaton

My father

Hungarian Jews (among them children) walking toward the gas chambers in Auschwitz - Birkenau.

My mother and me at Salzburg in 1950, a few months before I left as an immigrant for Canada

My mother and me in the Autumn of 1945

My mother at Grödig, Austria prior to leaving for Canada (Summer, 1951)

One of the last pictures of my mother, taken at Innsbruck, Austria where she spent the summer in the early 1970s

New Career In Canada

Tomorrow night's staff party of the College st. YMCA will be the Toronto debut for concert pianist Johanna Biener of Budapest, Hungary, who two decades ago was the musical toast of two continents.

Back in the late 20's, Mrs. Biener played in Montreal, Quebec and Windsor during a concert tour of North America. As the wife of a successful young lawyer, she had a luxurious home in Budapest, four servants, jewels and a smart wardrobe.

But that was yesterday. Then came the war and Mr. Biener's death. When the war ended, the Communists took over Mrs. Biener's homeland and confiscated her riches. Many of her friends began to disappear mysteriously. Then in April, 1950, Mrs. Biener dressed in peasant clothes and escaped to Austria where she joined her son and went into the American zone of Germany.

Last month, the former concert pianist arrived in Toronto and a week ago she landed a job behind the Coffee Corner on the first floor of the College st. "Y". She earns $25 a week plus free meals and as much coffee as she can drink.

Tomorrow's concert is but the start of what Mrs. Biener hopes may be a continuance of her musical career.

"Always I played the piano and people liked it," she said. "It can never be the same but I would like to give concerts once again. Perhaps I can teach too. It looks like we must start all over again."

A news clipping about my mother published by a Toronto daily in 1952

Erwin today

Part 3

Coming to Canada

On Board the Troop Ship

I have just realized that when I was on board of the cruise ship *"Emerald Princess,"* that I had hardly thought of my first sea voyage which I had made 58 years ago prior to that pleasurable Baltic cruise, early last summer. I should have remembered that earliest voyage because that was the first time I saw the ocean under entirely different circumstances.

It was on a stormy day that I embarked in the company of hundreds of Displaced Persons (or DPs) on the troop transport ship, *"USNS General Harry Taylor"* at the port of Bremerhaven. Most of us came by train from Austria up to that post city where we were temporarily housed in a DP camp.

Having a lot of time to kill we took walks around the once ornate Hanseatic city which we found quite dispiriting. There were still ruins everywhere, covered in parts by fresh spring foliage, which sprouted among the still stinking debris. Knowing that in about ten days or so I would be landing in Canada, I was filled by both hope and apprehension.

As soon as we got on deck of the troop ship we were led to our sleeping quarters. After descending on a circular staircase into the bowels of the ship we entered a huge sleeping area. There were innumerable rows of three-tiered bunks which once served the soldiers transported overseas and back to the US during and after the Second World War. I felt a bit frightened because I had never slept in the same room with hundreds of people. As soon as we lay down we heard three blasts from the deck, a signal that we were about to cast off from the pier. No more than half an hour could have passed when we began to hear the thunderous clash of waves against the hull of the ship, a terrible racket that continued throughout the night. Very soon I got pretty seasick and so did many others. When I woke up after a restless sleep I began to feel the acrid smell of vomit which lingered in the huge sleeping quarters. Almost no one felt like eating breakfast after that awful night.

At last I got onto my feet towards noon and made my way to the deck. As soon as I got there I was stopped by an officious looking man in a kind of nondescript uniform who asked me to go to an office at the aft of the vessel. It was there that we were assigned our chores for the duration of the voyage. As the ship had to be maintained and because as refugees in the care of the International Refugee Organization, we didn't have to pay for the passage, it was only fair that we were given all kinds of shipboard maintenance jobs.

I soon saw a group of my fellow passengers leaving with pails and brushes from one of the depots. They were directed by a burly crewman who, I thought, was going to show them how to paint the deck. Some women I spoke to were assigned to the kitchen and the laundry departments. I had the impression that practically every one of the hundreds of emigrants on board got busy doing the most varied physical chores, even while they felt still woozy after the stormy night.

The person who assigned the jobs was a very efficient non-nonsense Englishman –probably someone with a military background. He didn't need an interpreter when I came before him for I spoke fairly fluent English. When he asked me about my work experience I told him that I was working at the offices of the International Refugee Organisation as well as those of the American Joint as a DP until I left Salzburg to board the train for Bremen.

"Can you type?" he asked me.

"Yes," I answered, adding that apart from Hungarian I could also speak English and German.

"OK" he said. "I'll give you a job in the office."

I had the feeling that, unlike those assigned to do physical labour I had quite a cushy job. I had to formulate and type letters of recommendations day in and day out for those who had worked on the ship for future reference in the New World. The letter heads carried the emblem of "USS General Taylor" and on the bottom of the document I had to affix the stamp of the International Refugee Organization. Later I had to put the finished copies in alphabetical order for signature on the desk of the very businesslike Englishman. I was not too much bored with the job because I had to act as an interpreter to many of those who came to the office with their problems.

Despite the many hours that I spent doing clerical duties I had time enough to wander around the ship where, by the way, I ate my first American meal. I found the food on the whole rather indifferent, except for the ice cream which was wonderfully scrumptious and creamy compared to that I used to eat in the old country.

A few days before we reached our first port a number of emigrants organized a farewell concert. There were a few very talented dancers and musicians who put together a colourful program. There was also a very good amateur violinist from Prague who gave a fiery performance of Monti's famous *"Csardas."* (I had met the middle-aged man in Toronto where he could find a job only as a cleaner. I had heard later that unable to cope with his heavy duties, he hanged himself).

On the ninth day of the voyage, we finally reached Halifax. Coming ashore I was pretty disappointed. It was cold, foggy and rainy; I was shivering because I was completely unprepared after the beautiful spring in Europe for the half-wintry Canadian weather. When I had to sign some forms at the desk of an emigration officer, I suddenly realized that it was April Fools Day. Was this an April joke or the beginning of an interesting adventure? I kept asking myself before I boarded the night train which took us to Montreal.

General Labourer

It was around noon when a bunch of us, young immigrants, arrived with the train from Toronto at the Brantford railway station. We were led by our minders to the main platform where farmers all over the region were waiting for us. As soon as we got near them they started to feel us up to test our muscles for the heavy jobs waiting for us. I soon noticed that hardly any of our prospective employers approached me. They hardly looked at me and soon turned away to muster the other boys and men. Having selected their workers the rail way platform soon became empty. Obviously, I wasn't fit for this kind of labour and I began to wonder what was going to happen to me. Just when I thought that I am going to be left alone at this rural train station one of our minders approached and said: "Well, no luck. I have got to drive you to the Brantford Employment Office."

When we arrived he introduced me to a senior official who was supposed to solve the problem. He was a tall man, who it turned out was himself an immigrant. He told me that he came from Poland, via a number of Displaced Persons' camps, and promised to help me to get a farm job. After phoning around for a while he found the people who might need my help.

It was close to dinner time when we arrived at a large garden centre. After I said goodbye to the Pole who drove me something quite unexpected had happened Instead of letting me get to my quarters for a wash and a rest the manager of the centre ordered me to grab the next wheel barrow and empty the sand from it. I still don't know whether he wanted to test me or spite me in giving me this job. Whatever his motives, I spontaneously refused to carry out the job. I told him that I was tired and hungry and feeling as I did couldn't follow his order. He looked at me with anger and without a word left in a huff. A short while later, he came back and said that I had a phone call. When I took the receiver in one of the hothouses I heard an angry tirade. It was the manager of the Brantford Employment Office.

"You are an impudent brat to refuse the order of your employer" he said and added, "I am as much a Jew as you are and I know how your mind works".

I had no doubt that this was an oblique anti-Semitic statement and as it was the first one I had heard in Canada, I became frightened as well as angry. Whatever he had in mind, he had to get me back to his office because the people at the garden centre refused to have anything to do with me.

In half an hour or so, the Polish official arrived. He didn't seem to have been angered by my refusal.

He said "I am going to drive you to a Hungarian farmer who seems to be quite glad to hear that I'll bring him one of his compatriots."

It was after dark when we arrived at a large farm. We were received by an old Hungarian peasant, Uncle B, who told us that as a dirt-poor farm labourer, he had emigrated to Canada shortly after the First World War. It took him years of very hard work to buy a plot together with the rather big house he and his family were living in. He was lucky, he said, to live in the midst of the tobacco farm area, because tobacco brought in a lot of money after the yearly harvests in August and September. So he was able to lay a lot of dough aside and become established as a fairly prosperous farmer in the Delhi area.

Uncle B treated me that evening very well. He gave me a good Hungarian dinner and led me to a comfortable, small bedroom, where I could sleep very well.

I was wakened around six in the morning and after a good breakfast I was sent into the stable and asked to shovel manure into a wheel barrow. This turned out to be a very difficult job because I had neither the idea how to heap the manure into the shovel, nor how to handle the heavy wheel barrow. Having struggled with this job for a while, I heard the voice of Uncle B behind my back.

"I can see that you are quite unfit for farm labour, so it would be useless to employ you here," he said. "I think that you would be much better off working in an office than here on my farm".

He said this in a friendly tone and after a good lunch he drove me to the bus station and asked me to go back to the Brantford Labour Office.

I can still remember how frightened I was when I got on the bus in Delhi. What if I had to face that very unfriendly manager of the Employment Office again? Would he going to hand me over to the police for my refusal and inability to carry out the jobs I was ordered to do? And even worse, would I be deported back to Germany or Austria as a useless layabout? My only hope was to meet again the friendly Polish-Canadian official.

After finding my way to the Brantford Employment Centre, I couldn't but head right to his office. As a man more or less in charge of my job placement, he appeared to be somewhat disappointed. He must have felt that if he had sent me to yet another farm he would soon find me again back at his office.

After some thought he said, "I have got an idea which might help you." He took the phone and spoke to someone to whom he described my situation. Finishing the call he told me, "I have a good acquaintance, another Hungarian, who promised to take you in for a while. You can stay with him and his family in their Brantford apartment until you can extricate yourself from this unpleasant situation." (How I managed to do that is another story)

In any event, I was received like a relative by Mr L and his wife (both of them immigrants from Hungary), and stayed for more than a week with them in Brantford. I spent a lot of time walking around that city longing to be back in Europe again. But things turned out quite differently than had imagined. It was only seven years later, in 1958 that I returned to Europe. (I left Canada as a student to spend a good number of years at several European universities before I had returned to Toronto.)

Part 4

Back to Europe

The London Uncle

When I got off the train at Paddington railway station, it was the end of a long journey. I crossed the Atlantic in six days on board of a passenger liner. After the ship anchored at Plymouth harbor, I caught the train to London. Dead tired when I finally arrived, I was looking forward to a good meal and a long sleep in my uncle's London apartment.

This was the first time I had left Canada for Europe since I arrived at Halifax as an immigrant on a cold and rainy April day in 1951. My initial objective for going overseas was to change the course of my studies, for I felt pretty frustrated by the narrow analytic way philosophy was taught at the University of Toronto where I was studying for an Honours BA. Originally, I wanted to attend a German university, but my uncle dissuaded me from going to Freiburg or Heidelberg for reasons which at the time appeared to me convincing.

I immediately recognized my uncle who was waiting for me on the platform of Paddington train station. He looked very similar to how he appeared to me when he was still living in Hungary. He was a rather tall, somewhat bent, but still good-looking man in his early fifties. Unlike so many Hungarian Jews of bourgeois origin, he had left the country shortly after the Germans marched into Austria. He warned my father to follow suit, but dad felt safe enough not to become an immigrant. After all, he insisted, he had a very good position as the corporation lawyer of a big hydro company. A few weeks after we said goodbye to my uncle and his wife, my father showed us a newspaper report about my uncle's five year old son, Peter, who with a tag with his name and destination around his neck, left alone on an airplane from Budapest to join his parents in London.

As it was after dark when I arrived, I didn't see much of London on our way to my uncle's apartment. When he parked his car he told me that he lived in the Temple, a rather exclusive residential area. As a barrister, he continued, who has his chambers in this part of London reserved for the legal profession, he was permitted to have also his apartment there.

"It is in the very centre of London, a stone's throw away from Fleet Street and St. Paul's Cathedral. I'll show you around next morning," he said.

I was very much taken with the Temple during my uncle's conducted tour. He explained to me that it was one of the four Inns and Courts whose origins go back to the Middle Ages; they have the exclusive right to call candidates to practice law at the Bar of England and Wales. He showed me the famous Gothic Temple Church as well as the large and ornate Dining Hall of the Honourable Society of the Middle Temple which was constructed during the reign of Queen Elisabeth I in the middle of the 16th century. I was also very much impressed by the elegant red-brick buildings which contained the chambers of the barristers and their solicitors.

After our walk around the Temple, my uncle took me to his chambers which were only a short distance away from his apartment. We went straight to his study where he offered me a seat facing his desk. After questioning me about the problems I had run into in Canada, he launched into a long speech about the best way I could make it as an immigrant to England.

"Listen my boy," he said in his highly cultivated courtroom English. "What's most important is you should never let on that you are of Jewish origin. If someone asks you about your religious background you should say that you, (like me) was a student of the elite Lutheran Lycée of Budapest. You know very well how Jews are still regarded, even if they belong to the upper-middle class like myself."

He then gave me some advice how I should behave in the company of English people.

"What's most important, never ask any personal questions when you are in their company. The English are very much reserved and they would get flustered or angry when you try to get nearer to them."

He went on in this vein for a long time after which I had the impression that I was entering a closed society hedged around with many odd rules which I ought to learn if I were to get along with them.

During the first week with my uncle and aunt they gave me a guide book and sent me out to explore the landmarks of London as a tourist. I found many of the sights interesting, yet I wasn't as interested as my uncle and his wife expected me to be. Recalling these early days, I think that I felt pretty depressed. It was the atmosphere in their apartment which made my mood sink pretty low. There was something very distant and at the same time pretty conventional in the way my uncle and aunt communicated. Apart from receiving their advice of how to behave, all I heard was small-talk which made me pretty bored. I got so tired by their chit-chat that at times I fell asleep during the meals. Obviously, I couldn't but repress my feelings when I was talking with them. Yet, my uncle, unlike his wife, was a very intelligent and highly cultured person. He travelled widely, had a very rich library, and used to play the viola in amateur chamber music ensembles. I could only explain his reluctance to talk about interesting subjects by the fact that he was dog-tired when he arrived home from the courts or his chambers, for he was a terribly hard worker. Apart from working as an expert on international commercial law, he was also writing learned articles and publishing books about the legal powers of the UN. What's more, he was a Professor of Law at a red-brick university in southern England to which he commuted from London each Wednesday.

As my guardian - my "*in loco parentis*" as he used to say - he helped me financially with my undergraduate studies at the same university where he was lecturing. As a super achiever, he expected that I would perform much as he had. He told me many times that if I don't get a First, which would enable me to do my graduate studies in Oxford, I would have to find a job.

When after two years of study I ended up with a B in Philosophy, he told me, "Well my boy, that was a creditable performance."

He implied of course that I wasn't good enough to become an academic and would have to look for a position, possibly as a teacher in one of the English public schools. In fact, nothing came of this project and I had to earn my keep while I was in England until I got my compensation payment and monthly pension as a victim of the Holocaust from the Federal authorities of West Germany.

While in London, I met a student and assistant of the Marxist philosopher, George Lukacs. This youngish scholar had left Hungary after the 1956 revolution and, like me, was at the time attending a post-graduate seminar in Aesthetics at London University. One day, I told him a bit about my uncle, whose name was very well known by many Hungarians during the Cold War as a highly respected broadcaster and anti-Communist propagandist with the Hungarian service of the BBC.

I found his views about my uncle so striking that I jotted them down the same day in my diary. This is what he said:

"Your uncle is one of the many equilibrating devices of Capitalistic and late liberal society, a compromising specialist, a kind of legal technocrat. Instead of helping to destroy and create a new society, he acts very much like a repairman for the ancient regime."

What this very bright, dyed-in-the-wool Marxist said made me think, especially later when I was a student of Jürgen Habermas in Heidelberg, Germany. Reflecting about my uncle in much more nuanced terms, I found the views of this young Hungarian Marxist a bit too pat. I don't really believe that my uncle was simply "a repairman for the ancient regime." He in fact, held very strong liberal views, and moreover, he was a member of the English Law Reform Society, a body with strong links to the Fabian Society. According to Wikipedia the purpose of this Society "was to advance the principles of Democratic

Socialism, via a gradualist and reformist, rather than revolutionary means."

My uncle, who died when he was eighty, was far from a simple man and I am sure that he had a social conscience. I am certain that in his university lectures and through his work with the English Law Reform Society he was seriously set against the evils of Capitalism. One cannot deny, however, that he made a lot of money by defending the interests of large, international pharmaceutical companies. Still, I feel that it would be unfair to portray him with a broad Marxist brush because I am sure he saw the dangers of reckless Capitalism. Even though he treated me in a fairly harsh, often condescending manner, I owe him a lot because he enabled me to live and study in England which I have no doubt only enriched my life as a student.

The Art of Hitch-hiking

I was standing for at least three hours near the entrance of a highway near Karlsruhe waiting for a car to stop for me, desperately hoping that I would get away at last from that damned spot. I would have loved to be in Strasbourg before dark. It looked however, as if I would have to give up getting a lift in the direction to that city or anywhere that day. What else could I have done under the circumstances but to spend the night at a youth hostel? As a student living on a small allowance I didn't have the money for a hotel nor for a train ticket. The solution to see something of Europe in the 1950s and 1960s was therefore a rather popular but rather uncertain one: hitchhiking, or in the popular parlance of the day going by "auto-stop."

The first thing you needed to make the best of this uncertain mode of transportation was patience - and a well neigh inexhaustible one. If I had given up not far from Karlsruhe during that endless day, I would have missed the car which had finally picked me up. This means of course that patience would have to be paired with luck, that is to say, you had to believe to the very end in your luck; and if you failed that day you would trust that you would have a nice break the next one.

Another thing that would help to make your way free of charge through the highways of Europe was your sex. If you happened to be (preferably a good looking) girl or woman you had a much better chance of getting a lift than if you were a male. To take advantage of this situation, men often let their female companions stand alone at the edge of the road while they were hiding themselves behind trees or bushes. Once the car stopped for the girl, the man would suddenly emerge from where he was hiding and ask the driver if he could join his companion for the ride. I am sure that this trick had disappointed many a driver. To be a female and to be alone on the road was certainly not without risks. Some of these daring women had never made it back home, having been killed by murderous rapists. But many of them who made it were molested by motorists who believed that the ride with the lone woman would lead to a sexual adventure. (I know, however, one woman who all through her many auto stops managed to escape this kind of aggression, but for that you needed plenty of luck).

Last but not least, it usually helped to get a lift if you were travelling light. I saw many hitch-hikers with bulky knapsacks and sleeping bags having been turned down by drivers, especially by ones who had other persons riding in their car.

What I found particularly interesting, but also disturbing during my numerous rides, were the personalities of those who allowed me to join them in their cars. I soon realized that when alone during a long time with a total stranger people tend to be much more open than under normal circumstances. As a result, I heard many stories of considerable varieties and interests. Some were endless boasts, or political lectures which made me quite uncomfortable, but of course I didn't dare to antagonize the drivers because they were doing me a favour. I also heard desperate confessions, lachrymose, and angry stories of unrequited love.

Rare were the drivers who allowed me to engage in discussions and they turned out to be the most interesting ones. I will never forget the man who took me for a longish ride at the time when I was studying in England.

I had already waited for hours at the roadside near Ostend (Belgium) for a lift when finally a car stopped. Asking me where I was heading I told him that I would like to get eventually to Paris.

"Well, I can take you all the way to Cologne, but I have to stop at a hotel because it is already getting late," he said.

I readily agreed because I was almost certain that I wouldn't get another ride after dark. As soon as we got under way we started to talk. From the very first I felt that we were on the same wavelength. The man, as I soon found out, was a Belgian diplomat, who like me, was quite interested in both literature and the arts. What I remember best of our long discussion was that after an hour or so he started to sing after I told him about my love of twentieth century French composers.

"Do you like Fauré?" he asked.

"Yes" I said. "I love his Requiem."

"Then you would like this," he answered.

In a nice baritone he sang a rather plaintive, beautiful melody, I had never heard before. It was Fauré's *"Pavane,"* a song that had since become one of my favourites of the French repertoire.

When we reached Liège, not far from the German frontier, we parted way for the night. He drove me to a youth hostel before he drove to his hotel. As promised he picked me up early in the morning. When we arrived in Cologne he invited me for lunch at a restaurant near the Cathedral, where we continued our discussion. After we got up to leave we had to walk through a badly-lit passage. That's where he stopped and turned to face me.

"I really enjoyed your company, he said," and then quite unexpectedly brushed his hand ever so slightly over my crotch. I wasn't quite sure what he really meant, but I couldn't help thinking that he wasn't only intellectually but also erotically attracted to me. I had pretended not to have noticed this unusual gesture and we parted quite amicably after I told him how much I have enjoyed the ride.

There is one more episode of these low-budget cross-country trips that particularly stands out in my mind. I remember one hot summer morning when in the company of a young French woman I was waiting for a car to stop. I met her at a nearby youth hostel and we decided to make together the "autostop." We were waiting near a small town somewhere in Normandy trying to hitch a ride. We stood there for at least three hours while many cars raced past and it was rapidly getting dark. Hopeless as our situation had appeared, we were debating whether to call it a day and return to the youth hostel where we had met.

"OK, let's give it another quarter of an hour until it gets quite dark," I said. Although somewhat reluctant to accept my proposal, the girl finally gave in. Just as we were about to return to the youth hostel a car suddenly stopped. A woman opened the door and asked us where we would like to go. I said we would like to get to Paris.

"Well, I can take you as far as Evreux, if that's good enough for you," she said

Knowing as we did, that there would be another youth hostel in that town, we got into her car. She told us that she was a teacher at a lycée and was just returning home from her vacations. Tired as we were, we had a very animated discussion.

Just before she dropped us before the hostel she said, "You know, I saw you two standing at the roadside but I drove past. But the longer I drove the more I was thinking of you wondering what are you going to do in the dark. So after a good while, I made up my mind and I turned back to fetch you."

I asked her how long it had taken her to return to the spot where we were standing.

"Oh," she said, "perhaps a good twenty minutes or so."

I wished there had been more drivers who would have acted in such a selfless manner.

Heidelberg

It was a blustery, rainy November evening when I arrived from Victoria train station at Dover. Loaded with three bulky suitcases and a heavy travelling bag, I was struggling to get on board the ferry which was to take me to Ostend. I was on my way to Heidelberg, but had no idea how I was going to manage; changing trains twice with all my luggage before arriving at my destinations appeared to me a well-nigh impossible task.

As soon as we left the harbor the ferry ran into a heavy storm that left its mark on most of the passengers. Bouncing up and down with the ship they became violently seasick, seeking shelter on the benches or folding seats below deck. I, on the contrary, was in a much better condition than they, having taken a good dose of dramamine tablets an hour before I boarded the ship. As a result, I could spend a lot of time enjoying the fresh sea air on deck rather than moving down to the tightly sealed, vomit-reeking compartments.

Why did I wish to leave London and continue my studies in Heidelberg? It was a matter of sheer coincidence, an unexpected encounter in Burgundy that had prompted me to leave England behind and make a new start as a graduate student in Germany.

When I was in France in the early 1960s, I became fascinated by Romanesque architecture after I visited the *"Abbaye aux Hommes*" (Men's Abbey) in Caen, built shortly after the Norman Conquest. I was fascinated by its bulky structure resembling a fortress, its crypt and its imposing, long cloisters. I loved this highly symmetrical, defensively built architecture which fed my fantasy of the Middle Ages. Advised by an art historian acquaintance of mine to visit Burgundy to look at the most impressive examples of Romanesque churches and cathedrals, I hitch-hiked to the area to view these striking edifices. On the way, I met a German student who, like me, was trying to hitch a ride down to this beautiful hilly region of France.

Christian L, who studied theology at the University of Heidelberg, was a very learned young man. Walking with him through Vézelay Cathedral was a real pleasure because, well-versed in Christian iconography, he explained to me the meaning of the many biblical scenes sculpted on the capitals of this remarkable, romanesque devotional structure. He also aroused my interest in telling me a great deal about the theory of interpreting texts - Hermeneutics

– whose study was one of the focal points of the Philosophy Department of the University of Heidelberg. Dissatisfied as I was with the analytically-oriented philosophy curriculum that prevailed at the time at British Universities, I felt that a change to Heidelberg would be in my best interest. The fact that Christian promised to help me to get through the initial hurdles after my arrival at his university was an additional factor that encouraged me to move to Heidelberg as soon as I could manage to leave London.

It was well after midnight when I boarded the train at Ostend and dawn was breaking when I arrived in Heidelberg. Lugging my heavy suitcases, I somehow made my way to the station building where, at this early hour, almost everything was closed except a wonderfully equipped bath room for travellers. How pleasurable it was to immerse myself in the hot water after the all night train journey!

Two things struck me when I stepped out from the station building on this cold November morning. The first was the angry shout of a policeman. He was bellowing at me because I crossed over to the streetcar stop at a point which was apparently forbidden to pedestrians. This was not the best welcome to Germany, considering the grotesquely threatening image of Wehrmacht sergeants. What was much more pleasant, though a bit unusual was the smoky wintry smell which the sharp wind wafted over the city. Even though this was a far cry from the spring scent of opening flowers, its wintry aroma became indelibly associated with my first and many other days that I spent as a graduate student on the shores of the Neckar.

Thanks to Christian L, I didn't have to look for digs when I arrived that morning. He reserved a room for me at one of the students' residences, an unexpected boom for someone completely unfamiliar with the layout of the city and the housing situation for university students. What I noticed first when I moved into one of the tall buildings was that it overlooked a stretch of fields as far as the eye could see. It was great to be so near to the countryside and also quite convenient living fairly close to the university.

Despite having lived at a students' hall in England, life at the Student's residence in Heidelberg was strangely unfamiliar to me. The more time I had spent in the *"Studentenwohnheim I am Klausenpfad,"* the more my life at the two student residences appeared so different to me. Living with students under the same roof in England was on the whole quite a casual affair; apart from wearing gowns in the dining hall which was presided over by the master of the college and members of the teaching staff at the High Table, there were no special rules there. On the whole, we could live a fairly unrestricted way unless we committed some serious offence.

In contrast, life at "*Klausenpfad*" was quite a different affair. I soon noticed that we were hedged in by rules which specified our behaviour in a strange manner. To ensure that these rules were kept, the governing students of the residence established a tribunal which meted out various punishments. For lesser offences there were several warnings that could lead to expulsion if they were three times repeated. The most serious of them concerned "illegal" behaviour between the sexes. While sleeping with your boy or lady-friend at the residence was allowed from 8AM until 11PM, all cohabitation during the night was considered a very grave offence for which people were immediately expelled. I think that this rule was as silly as it was hypocritical, for it would appear that having a tryst after certain hours with someone amounted to shacking up with a person in the eyes of the student law-givers. I remember repeated occasions when this so called "11PM paragraph" was strictly punished. And yet there were a lot of students who simply risked the consequences of "illegal" sex. You only had to be careful not to have enemies who would take pleasure in reporting you to the student tribunal.

Talking of "illegal" sex, there was one case that became a real scandal at the time. What happened wasn't simply between students but between the wife of the head of our residence and one of the students who resided in our section on the fifth floor. He was an intelligent medical student who seduced the wife of the university appointed head of the residence, and ran away with her and their little daughter. This created a terrible stink that after a few weeks ended when the guilt-stricken wife had returned with her child to her cuckolded husband. The offending student ended up before the university disciplinary body and was sent down by them. (As far as I remember he was able to continue his studies at another university and became later a physician).

I spent two years at Heidelberg until Professor Jürgen Habermas got the chair of Philosophy at Frankfurt University to where I had followed him with all of his other graduate students.

I loved staying in Heidelberg for a number of reasons. It was a beautifully located smallish city, very close to the picturesque countryside. I particularly loved walking on the famous *"Philosophenwe"* - the Philosopher's Walk - overlooking the ancient centre of the city with its many historical buildings. I often continued for many miles on this famous path which runs parallel to the Neckar. An acquaintance of mine pointed out during one of our walks that one of the islands of this river had become the residence of many retarded people. They had for centuries led incestuous lives, he said. As we walked he said, pointing to a very odd-looking hunchbacked elderly man, that the one sitting on a bench near the island was one of them. This sounded to me as an urban legend, but I have neglected to find out if there was really an "idiots' island" a walking distance from the city.

As I am very much interested in art, I frequently visited the gallery of the psychiatric clinic of the University, where one of the richest collections of the graphic works of mentally ill patients are to be found. Founded by the psychiatrist and art historian Hans Prinzhorn, I spent many hours looking at these strangely fascinating images of "mad" patients, some of whose paintings or drawings I think would deserve to be shown in major art galleries.

Unlike Frankfurt and Mannheim, Heidelberg completely escaped the raids of allied bombers. While the two other cities were terribly devastated, the latter seemed to have enjoyed an immunity from allied aerial attacks. It is said that the good fortune of this beautiful city is largely due to American and British students who once studied there and rose later to influential positions in the army and airforce. It is suggested that this enabled them to save the city from the terrible fate of many other German cities.

There is a famous kitchy song, "*Ich habe mein Herz in Heidelberg verloren*" – "I lost my heart in Heidelberg." Could it be that these military men had loved Heidelberg so much (or loved so much some girl or woman there) that they did everything to save the city? Who knows maybe there is some truth in this legend.

A Memorial Service

I am in the music room of a rich amateur musician in a lavish home in the Taunus mountains, near Frankfurt. A memorial service is about to begin for the mother of Herr Dr M. The casket is placed next to the pipe organ and soon the ceremony is about to begin.

How did I get there? And what were my connections to this upper-middle class German family? To fill in the gaps I must go back to the mid-nineteen sixties when I was a student at Frankfurt University and lived in the same village where the family M. were residing.

When I was in Heidelberg, my mother decided to come over from Canada and stay with me for a while in Germany. When I finally had to move to Frankfurt to follow my professor, who was offered the chair of philosophy there, my mother got to know Herr Dr M and his family through sheer chance. It so happened that at the time a close Canadian friend of my mother

Mrs L was attending a congress in Germany with the wife of Dr M. She introduced my mother to her German friends who offered my mom a position as a companion to the mother-in-law of the wife of Mr M. In retrospect this would appear quite a problematic job because the twice-married Mrs K was a difficult, cranky old woman: at the time, however, my mother was ready to accept it because she, as a pianist, was attracted to the musical culture of the household.

It was at a musical soirée when I visited the home of Herr M for the first time . When I arrived there were already a lot of people waiting for the *"Hauskonzert"* to begin. They were mostly middle-aged and elderly people, members of the cultured German middle-class. I might have been wrong, but I couldn't help but sense a devotional atmosphere in the large music room. It was the quasi-religious, deadly serious way this older generation related to music and literature which was often rooted in a profound conservatism.

The concert was very enjoyable, considering that two of the performers were professional musicians and Dr M himself - an amateur - was a very competent pianist. Herr G, a noted professor of voice at the Frankfurt conservatory had a fine baritone voice; the alto who joined him later in duets, a lady who said that she was of half-German and half red-Indian origin, was a bit too dramatic for my taste. After the concert I enjoyed the fine sandwiches and the drinks offered by the hostess. It seems that most of the people who had been invited knew each other, but I who was there for the first time, found it difficult to join the conversation because I felt like an outsider surrounded by these *"Bildungsbürger"* - culturally conscious members of the German middle class.

What also held me back from mingling with these people was my suspicion that at least some of them had been supporters, if not Party members, of the Third Reich. It was common knowledge that Dr M himself, was a member of the Party, but like so many others, he changed over after the war to the governing Christian Democratic Party. One thing I knew, I would never tell them anything about my Jewish origins if they had ever asked me about my family background.

Compared to the opportunistic Dr M, his wife was an out-and-out idealist. She believed in higher social causes, was an ardent member of an international organization of democratic women and more often than not tended to be quite effusive. I don't quite know how husband and wife got along, but it's quite certain that Mrs M and her mother-in-law hated one another. My mother, who used to be the companion of the old lady, had witnessed certain scenes between the two which revealed the poisonous nature of this ugly relationship.

As my mother had been a permanent house-guest of the family for about two months, I used to visit her as often as I could at the M's. They lived in a rather comfortable but rambling home surrounded by a never-ending, largely uncultivated field. When I saw my mother there for the first time, she told me, "Go to the toilet on the ground floor and you are going to have a surprise."

First there was nothing surprising about this finely scented lavatory. But when I started to roll the toilet paper I heard the jingling chimes of a musical clock which played a well-known tune from an Italian opera.

What I enjoyed most in the house was to play the instruments of the music room to which both my mother and I had (at least while Dr M was away) free access. Apart from the house organ there was also a concert grand and a cembalo in the room. I loved to play on all three instruments experimenting with different keyboard techniques, which was really great fun. My mother herself was overjoyed practicing on the Steinway grand -and I suspect that this was the main reason why she accepted her strange and at times difficult job with the family.

After my mother returned to Canada, I stopped visiting the M's except on one last occasion. This was when I received an invitation to attend the memorial service for Mrs K who had died a few days earlier. As I looked around the music room, I saw the closed casket of the old lady placed on a special dais next to the organ. Seeing the heavy oak coffin with its two brass handles, I suddenly recalled my last meeting with the deceased. She was already quite weak, yet she insisted on attending a song recital at the nearby spa. As I was also interested in the program I offered to accompany her, which she readily accepted. She told me on the way how glad she was to have had my mother as her companion.

"It was so good to have her because I feel quite isolated on account of my continuous fights with my daughter-in-law," she said. "I wish your mother would come back because I can hardly stand the aggravation which makes me even sicker than I am."

Soon after the first number, Mrs K started to cough. I thought that she would soon stop, but she was unable to control herself. Her attack, which I later found out was due to severe asthma, got so bad that we had to leave the concert after the third number.

Now, listening to the devotional Bach choral played during the memorial service by her son Dr M, and then hearing the solemn address by the pastor of their church talking about this happy, exemplary German family, I was wondering how many people who knew the Ms would have believed what was being said. And suddenly I had a fanciful idea. What if the deceased, thanks to supernatural powers, would have listened in to all the praise that was showered on her and her family? Incensed by all this fulsome bullshit she might have started to bang the sides of her coffin with her skeletal fists.

Buchenwald

For many years I had a strange, recurring dream. I dreamed that I was an inmate of a Nazi concentration camp. There was one thing that I found particularly disturbing in this nightmare. While I knew that the US Army was closing in on the area, I felt that I would never come out from that camp alive. On waking up I often imagined that if in these eerie dreams, the SS had shot me or forced me with others into the gas chambers, I probably would have been found dead the next morning, carried away by a stroke or a heart attack.

I had no trouble understanding why I had been plagued for so many years by this nightmare. While unlike so many other Jews, I had never landed in any of the concentration camps, I was almost killed by the murderous Hungarian Arrow-Crossmen during the Holocaust. No wonder that the fantasy of dying in one of the Nazi hell holes had haunted me for such a long time.

When I was in Weimar to do research on the famous diarist and great German patron of the arts, Harry Graf Kessler, I knew that I was a stone's throw away from Buchenwald. In fact, it was in a beautiful area, on a picturesque wooded mountain north of the city - the *Ettersberg* - that the Nazis had chosen as the venue of that dreadful concentration camp. And it was in those same woods that Goethe and other writers and thinkers loved to take their walks at the time when Weimar had become one of the centres of the German Enlightenment.

Reluctant, as I first was, to visit the memorial site of Buchenwald, I made up my mind one morning to take the bus up to the *Ettersberg*. What struck me on the way to the top where the camp was located, was the beauty of those light-coloured beech woods. But soon, like ugly, stubby fingers, the longish, squat buildings of the one-time SS barracks appeared - sixteen of them built in the ugly, Germanic country-house style of the Third Reich. There was a sinister monotony about these edifices which, when I saw them, housed many families who had moved up there on account of the lack of living quarters in and around Weimar. I was wondering how people felt living in these mass-produced, tan-coloured, three story, renovated barracks, so close to the one-time concentration camp. But I imagine that sooner or later, they got used to them for sake of convenience.

I deliberately avoided joining tour groups which were guided around the camp. Having read a number of books about Buchenwald, I was determined to walk through the camp grounds without the company of anyone else. I wanted to shut out any learned interference or conversations because at that memorial area I wanted to be with my thoughts and emotions by myself.

I visited the prison, the so called "bunker" where so many inmates in tiny cells were tormented by specially trained guards. I saw a contraption, camouflaged as a wooden rod for seemingly measuring the unsuspecting victims' height while an SS man shot them in the nape of their necks through an adjustable opening from behind. I saw the surgical tables where the inmates were experimented on by SS physicians with the special drain to remove the accumulated blood flowing from the "patients" veins. I also walked through the crematorium with its sturdy ovens where thousands of bodies were burned. Later, I went to see the site of the quarry at the edge of the forest where so many prisoners were worked to death. Last but not least, I visited the huge storage building, the so called *"Effektenkammer"* where the personal belongings of the prisoners used to be kept and which had been converted to a special museum by the authorities of the so called German Democratic Government. Apart from the discarded clothing of the inmates, what I saw there was an exhibition designed to celebrate the resistance movement of the Communist inmates. It was arranged to show the heroism of the comrades as the most compelling feature of Buchenwald's life. What surprised me was that I could find hardly any sign in this expo of ordinary prisoners, except the images and the instruments of clandestine Communist conspirators planning to sabotage the camp.

Before visiting the camp, I was told not to miss the huge memorial commissioned by the authorities of the German Democratic Republic as their tribute to those who suffered and died in Buchenwald. Following the signs, I walked down through the forest for about ten-fifteen minutes when I saw through the trees a tall, squat tower dominating the grounds of the memorial. With its strange rows of columns superimposed on top of it, it made me think of a mausoleum. It was the belltower from which at certain intervals the chimes of the funeral bells were to be heard. On a large pedestal, just in front of this tall, ugly edifice, I saw a group of sculptures which were conceived according to the motto, "Through Death, and Armed Struggle to Victory." The figures that I was looking at represented ideas rather than the artistic semblance of living experience. Falling, rising and gesticulating they were designed to symbolize ideological conceptions about the struggle, resistance and final victory of the Communists imprisoned in the camp. All I could see was sculpted rhetoric in the service of a calcified ideology. This memorial was also intended as a *"Mahnstätte"* - "Grounds of Reminder," which were no doubt utilized by Party propagandists to point to signs of "rising Fascism" in the Federal Republic of Germany.

There was something terribly grim and claustrophobic about the whole area with its fortress-like walls and eighteen huge block-like steles, each dedicated to the citizens of eighteen countries who were deported to Buchenwald. The very monumentality of this conception with its thick ring of walls, reminded me of certain funeral memorials, the so called "fortresses of the dead," favoured by conservative as well as Nazi architects.

Oppressed by this propaganda paean to the victims of the camp, I felt relieved when I entered again the woods of the *Ettersberg*. But rather than walking back to the parking area to catch the bus back to Weimar, I decided to take a last walk around the camp. I felt strangely moved when I looked again at the many broken bricks which were scattered where once of the prisoners' barracks had stood. Having just seen the pompous memorial grounds, the sight of these remnants of terror and suffering made me think of the many victims whose tortures cannot be expressed by words, let alone propagandistic memorials.

I suddenly remembered an episode in one of the books of Jorge Semprun, who himself was a prisoner in the camp. That's where he met his old teacher, the noted sociologist, Maurice Halbwachs who was dying of dysentery. Unable to talk, covered in his own excrements, he still seems to understand a line from a famous poem of Baudelaire that Semprun recites to him:

"Ô Mort, vieux capitaine, il est temps! Levons l'ancre.
Ce pays nous ennuie, ô Mort! Appareillons!"

"O Death, old navigator, the hour has come! Let us weigh anchor!
O Death, we are weary of this land, let us spread sail."

Part 5

Other Writings

The Nannies and the Governess

I remember the day when my grandpa asked one of my nannies, Adele, “Why is a button missing from the jacket of my grandson? Didn’t you see it and why didn’t you sew it on?”

When she said that I have probably torn it off, grandpa turned to me.

“Is this true, Erwin?” he asked.

Even though I knew full well that I had torn it off, I flatly denied that I removed the missing button. Grandpa, who was a terrible autocrat, fired the nanny on the spot because he thought that he had caught her lying.

I was a terribly spoiled little brat, an only child, who hated that middle-aged and very strict Austrian nanny. So I had no compunctions lying to my grandpa, which I greatly regret today.

I cannot overestimate the influence that some of those nannies had on me. While my parents were mostly concerned with their professional and social lives I spent most of the time in the company of these women who were charged to take care of me. The first one I remember was Anna, a simple, very affectionate person to whom I was very much attached. She was the one who inspired me to recite her name when I could still hardly talk. I used to say "Anna, Anna, Anna, Anna,/ Anna, Anna, Anna Anna," first going up and then down with my squeaky voice in a kind of singsong.

After this motherly Hungarian woman I was entrusted to the care of various German and Austrian *"Fräuleins"* most of whom I have forgotten. One day when I was about five, I made a remarkable discovery. I suddenly I realized that I could talk German. While I am sure that I had already more than an inkling of that language I will never forget that day when I felt certain that I was speaking German.

There was one *"Fräulein"* I still very much remember. She was a beautiful young, blond woman. Her name was Eva and she came from Hamburg. She smelt sweet and I loved to snuggle myself against her. It was great fun going with her day after day to a nearby park where we would play various games or listen to her reading from illustrated German children's books.

But she didn't stay in my company in that park all the time. She left me alone on certain days for a longish time telling to play on while she was visiting certain people. I sneaked after her a few times and noticed that she would enter the side door of the agricultural museum, a huge edifice which was fashioned after an old XIVth century castle. Even though I found her visits a bit strange I didn't worry about her frequent absences because, as usual , I was fully occupied by flying my little canvas airplane or playing with other kids in and around the rose-garden of the park.

One morning I found Eva packing her suitcases. When I asked her where she was going she said she had to go back to Hamburg because her mother was very ill. I felt terribly sad about her departure and asked my mother whether the *Fräulein* would come back.

"I very much hope so, but I can't tell to you when," she said.

As I found out much later my mother kept the whole truth about Eva's hasty departure from me. What she told me was an entirely different story.

"I noticed one day that she was getting pregnant," my mother told me when we were talking after the war about my children's maids. "The girl was in tears when I asked her about her condition. She said that she had an affair with the very good looking driver of the director of the Museum. I could do nothing but write her family informing them of what had happened. They phoned me a few days later and asked me to send her back to

Hamburg. It's a pity what had happened because I was quite fond of her."

Putting two and two together, I immediately understood what these strange visits to the side-entrance of the agricultural museum had meant.

There was another German woman whom my parents engaged when I was already nine years old. Unlike the others, she was no children's maid. She didn't live with us but visited me each afternoon and was hired as a kind of governess. Her name was Franziska and she came from Berlin. She spoke a very different, educated German unlike her predecessors. I loved her *"Hochdeutsch"* accent which I preferred to the very soft Austrian one. I loved her company because I had the feeling that she was the first of these foreign women who took me really seriously. We could talk about topics the others had never touched on. We looked for instance at a large English album about the First World War and she commented with insight and compassion on the many photos that she had shown to me.

My parents greatly appreciated this very companionable and intelligent woman because they noticed how much my German had improved thanks to her.

When I was in fourth grade I fell ill with tuberculosis and as a result Francisca had to stop visiting me. After I had recovered I saw her only twice.

The first time was at an outdoor swimming pool where I used to go almost every day during the summer. I was overjoyed to meet her and it seemed that she also enjoyed seeing me again. She told me she had to go back to Berlin on business but she had come back to Budapest mainly to avoid the bombing raids in Germany. I was surprised to see her in the company of a large boy who appeared to be in his late teens.

“This is my son,” she said. “I have managed to get him over for a short vacation in Hungary where he at least can have decent food.”

I was so fond of this woman that I asked for her local address which she readily gave to me. As she had no phone I decided a few months later to drop in on her unannounced. When I rang her door bell several times no one responded. On a sudden whim I turned the door handle which gave way. I entered a very dark corridor and noticed a half-open door. I called her name, but there was no answer. When I entered I saw her asleep with another man lying next to her in the bed. Seeing her in this unusual position I became so frightened that I turned on my heels and left the house as quickly as I could. For some reason I never breathed a word about what I saw that day.

I still keep wondering why I had kept silent. I think that I felt so close to this very kind woman, whose company I had enjoyed so much, that I couldn’t but keep my secret.

The Force of Music

One May day many years ago our music teacher at the Lutheran Lycée in Budapest put his hand over my rapidly-beating heart.

Pushing me from the wings toward the stage, he said, “Go out and play, I am sure you will do quite well”

I was to be the first and youngest performer at the annual concert at the ornate auditorium of our school. I was to play a sonatina by Mozart for which mother had prepared me months on end.

After the concert she said, “Your father and I sat trembling next to each other until you finished the piece.”

Remembering my stage fright as well as my effort to put everything into that sonatina, I can't help thinking how much I gained from the musical talents of my mother who was hoping that one day I would become a pianist, like herself.

As a small boy I would spend many hours near my mother while she was practicing her repertoire. She was an accomplished pianist and chamber music player who couldn't let a day go past without playing her instrument. Even though I liked listening to her she went to considerable lengths to bring closer the music to me. She would embroider what she was playing by inventing scenes that aroused my imagination.

I especially remember her scenarios for certain Beethoven Sonatas which had pride of place in her repertoire. *"Sunsets", "The Hermit"* and *"Witches Dances"* still stand out in my mind when I hear these pieces. As a result, I became keen on inventing scenarios myself listening to her music. When, for instance, she was playing one of the *"Ballades"* of Chopin I associated the piece with the scene of the great Gobelin tapestry that was hanging near the piano. Through the music the knights on their horses and the ladies surrounding them became alive to me. In my mind's eye they were leaving for an exciting hunt to the nearby forests. I imagined hearing the yelping of the dogs and the lusty shouts of the hunters. Trite as these scenarios may appear to sophisticated music lovers, I believe that the association of music with imaginary scenes only helped to develop my sensibility which later played a considerable role in my efforts to interpret various pieces.

When mother came to Canada as an immigrant she had a very tough time. Despite her talents, she had to take menial jobs like so many others from the old country. First she was employed as a seamstress at a small sweat shop. Then she became a scullery maid at one of the colleges of the university. At the same time I too had to earn my living the hard way, doing among other things, shiftwork at a metal wares factory.

My mother's position improved a bit when she found a job at the local YMCA coffee corner. There she met a number of people who took an interest in her. She was even interviewed for one of the local newspapers. Even though the reporter gave a full account of her privileged family background and her qualifications as a pianist, unfortunately this unexpected publicity had no practical effects. She continued to struggle at odd jobs (including the terribly tedious and very tiring job as a piano player at a ballet school) until something quite unexpected had happened.

One evening I decided to go to the movies. When I entered the lobby of the theatre I was surprised to see that the walls were hung with a lot of paintings. They were mostly fine watercolours which aroused my interest. When I saw the artist I got into a conversation with him and I soon learnt that he was a Scotsman who spent a lot of time in Germany and spoke the language as a native. When he asked me about my background, I also told him a lot about my mother and especially about her difficulties to get herself a job that suited her talents. As he himself used to study with the famous German pianist Walter Gieseking, he showed considerable interest in my mother. I invited him to come to see us because I knew that she would love to meet someone with similar artistic and cultural interests.

I was not surprised when mother and our guest started to talk music soon after I introduced one to the other. It was quite a spirited conversation about various famous pianists that the two had admired. It was the first time in Canada that my mother had talked to someone whose company she really enjoyed. When the Scotsman asked her to sit down and play him something, she readily obliged. As she was fortunate enough to have bought an old upright and as a result she was able to practice after she came home for work, she played quite beautifully that evening.

After she got up from the piano her visitor told her, “It so happens that I have a friend who is about to retire as a piano teacher. If I told him how good you are I am sure he would entrust you with his pupils.”

My mother readily accepted this completely unexpected offer. As the teacher had a lot of pupils it meant that she now would be able to earn her living as a piano teacher.

From my room in our tiny apartment I could often hear the way my mother was training the young boys and girls who came to her for their piano lessons. It was the way she spoke and sang while training her pupils which must have established a bond between her and them. I think that it was a spontaneous transfer of emotions from teacher to pupils which enabled them to grasp the essence of the pieces that they were learning. This didn't mean that they were simply aping my mother. She gave them enough leeway to also develop their own ideas of interpretation - provided they were musical enough to do so. As a proof of my mother's qualities as a teacher her pupils won many prizes at the annual Kiwanis music competitions.

Apart from being an excellent pedagogue, she was also an accomplished chamber music player. In her later years she was sought after by a number of amateur ensembles who invited her to play the piano parts in trios and quintets.

One hot June afternoon in the early nineteen-seventies I received a phone call. It was a lawyer, one of her chamber music partners, who urgently wanted to talk to me.

He said when I took the receiver, "Erwin, your mother has just suffered a heart attack and she was taken to the emergency department of the Western Hospital." I rushed with my wife to where she was transported. She lay in a large ward with other women. Even though we hoped that she would survive the completely unexpected coronary attack she died suddenly two days later.

A day after her death I spoke with the person who called me on that June afternoon. He told me that she got suddenly sick after she played the last chord of the piano part in Schubert's *"Trout Quintet."* I believe that in her enthusiasm she put all her emotions and energy into this beautiful work. But her heart - which must have been getting weaker for quite a while - just couldn't take her tremendous efforts as a musician any longer.

The First Five Minutes of a Recital

I heard an extremely interesting interview with the well-known Czech pianist Ivan Moravetz on CBC's Stereo Morning a few days ago. He talked about a rather exciting phenomenon, the importance of the first five minutes during a recital. According to Moravetz, the performer faces in this critical period, "a complicated situation. You hit the first note and there is a response. The way people respond represents a psychical attack on the player because they watch you and really the public eats you by their eyes and ears."

What the pianist suggests is that you have to establish the start of a rapport with the audience right from the start. Tom Duncan, who interviewed the artist, suggested that during these critical moments the performer has to function so to say on 'automatic pilot.' I think this is an excellent metaphor because it signifies a suspension of fears, apprehensions and compunctions. Thus, instead of anticipating unknown disasters, you let the music 'come freely to you.' Moravetz himself believes that, "in such blessed states the music plays by itself." He even ventures to call such privileged moments, "states of inspiration."

At the risk of sounding awfully pretentious, I believe that I have a sense of what he is talking about. For I have often experienced the agonizing flutter of the first minutes which can make or break a performance. Even before hitting the first note in a highly charged atmosphere, you should do your best to let those incalculable forces become an additional source of inspiration. Otherwise, they will come to you as so many threats and uncertainties that you would be lost reflecting on your ways of attacking the piano during those critical moments. In Moravetz's words, "that's when you are defending yourself against your own feelings and judgements."

On the other hand, if the artist lets the music really speak for itself, a good audience will also be carried by the spontaneous flow of the music. What's more, I believe their rapt participation will add so much more excitement to the performance. I am certain that a great artist feels quite intuitively when such 'blessed states' arrive. Such communications call of course for an ideal audience, an audience which I fear is becoming exceedingly rare in these days of stereomania.

If it is true what the pianist Ivan Moravetz suggests, it would appear that the artist and the audience 'create' a performance and therefore they are, at least to a certain extent dependent on one another. Thus a fidgeting, distracted audience can easily jolt the artist out of his composure. Conversely, the compunctions and hesitations of an artist could totally upset his performance even in the presence of the most receptive audience.

What Moravetz suggests, but never really gave a more detailed account during the interview, is the interdependence between the artist and the concert goers. What emerges as a result of this interplay is something like a medium which I believe can only be captured when one is present during a concert. On the other hand, when I am listening to a CD of an excellent live concert all I can do is to try to recreate the vibrant atmosphere which was very much present during the actual performance. The closest I can get to it, though this is no more than an artificial approximation, is during the first hearing of that CD. On second or third hearing I largely anticipate what is to follow and therefore even the semblance of a living contact will be lost forever.

I am not saying of course that a fine performance on a disc will not thrill the listener. Indeed, you can have a very profound musical experience next to your CD player. A superb recorded performance may even become a veritable source for musical discoveries. Yet, what can never be transposed onto it is the brittle, living presence of the audience in a concert or recital hall which together with the playing of the artist constitutes in a mysterious way the performance.

The Red and the White

A few days ago I saw an extraordinary film by the Hungarian director Miklos Jancso entitled, *"The Red and the White."* Set during the Russian Civil War, it shows the changing fortunes of the Bolsheviks and their Tsarists opponents, focusing on the fate of a group of Hungarians fighting with the Reds. The film has no plot in the ordinary sense and there are no heroes as bigger-than-life characters. What we see is the aftermath of minor skirmishes which result in the killings of captured opponents. In a sense the whole film us about the whims of the winners inflicted on the losers. Shooting soldiers in cold blood just because they fought at the other side becomes a mere routine. The more or less mechanical killing is at times entirely dependent on the mood and personality of those in charge of the various detachments. The decision to finish someone off or spare him shows the absurd cruelties of war in this film from an unusual angle. These barbarous scenes bring to light a deadly sense of contingency that stretches the nerves of the audience Every one of the episodes is played out in the most casual manner, for emotions have no visible place in the deadly games of the executioners in which most of the victims submit puppet-like to the bullets aimed at the nape of the neck.

Nowhere is the absorbing and harrowing rule over life and death in the film more evident that in the scenes involving women. The cruelty here is even more senseless because they, terrorized by the omnipotent commanders and their soldiers, take no active part in the short and sharp engagements raging in the steppes along the Volga. In one episode a peasant woman is humiliated by a young Cossack horseman. He orders her to undress. Resigned to her fate, she obliges. The Cossack obviously enjoys these preliminaries to sexual violence and takes his time in humiliating his victim by looking at her with voyeuristic pleasure. We in the audience follow with apprehension this cruel scene trying to imagine how the young soldier is going to have his pleasure and then dispose of the helpless woman. But at the moment when he is about to have his way with her, she is liberated by the commander of a White detachment who sentences the Cossack to death for his ghastly behaviour and has him killed on the spot.

There is an even more chilling scene that shows the cruel game of an almighty officer with a group of nurses working in a field hospital crammed with Red and White wounded soldiers. Knowing, as we do, that neither side spares their prisoners we suspect that the officer had come to threaten and punish the nurses for caring and giving shelter to the enemy. He commands the women to follow his totally inscrutable orders. At one point they are instructed to fish out the corpses of executed soldiers from a shallow river. Soon afterwards they have to line up in a row, a command that strongly suggest that they would be shot in short order. All this happens at a snail's pace, which only raises the apprehension of the audience. But then something completely unexpected happens: instead of being massacred the women are driven to a birch forest and asked to leave their carriages and walk through the shimmering grove of slender birch trees. Suddenly a marching band appears consisting of ragged soldiers. At a sign from the commander they strike up a medley of marches and melancholy waltzes. As if this wouldn't be enough, the officer asks the nurses in an exceedingly courteous manner to dance for him together. Slowly, with considerable hesitation the women form into couples and start moving to the music. Soon, however, they are swept along to the seductive rhythm of the waltzes which they perform with considerable grace under the glittering array of the slender birch trees.

It would be tempting to say that this mesmerizing scene is entirely out of place in a movie which depicts the senseless horrors of the Russian Civil War. Yet the astounding dance in the midst of unrelenting death and destruction reveals a mythic element, a "terrible symmetry" and a grotesque ecstasy which is very much the foil for this horrible and grotesque war. Jancsó excels in contrasting the beauties of nature with the most gruesome and cruel scenes through his superb black and white pictures. In trying to understand the unusual aesthetic power of his cinematic approach I keep remembering one of the most spectacular episodes of the film. Encircled by the overwhelming force of the Whites, a band of Reds, belonging to a Hungarian detachment sets out on a final, desperate attack. They march slowly and deliberately against four rows of Tsarist infantry men who stand rigidly arrayed. The Hungarian fighters, clad only in white shirts, approach the enemy while singing the Marseilles. It take an eternity till they raise their rifles to fire at the first two rows of the Whites who curiously just keep standing at ease without engaging the Reds. The shots hit their targets killing a number of the Tsarist soldiers who fall over like tin soldiers. When the attackers get closer, the Whites start firing in a deadly, concentrated manner, bringing down gradually the small but fearless band of Hungarian Reds.

Watching this scene brought to mind the useless heroes of other, suicidal attacks, the attacks of the

"Light Brigade" in the Crimean war, the absurdly costly British offensive at the Somme and last but not least, the legendary attack of the Polish Lancers against the invading panzers of the Wehrmacht at the beginning of the Second World War.

Considering that *"The Red and the White"* was made in 1967 to commemorate the fiftieth anniversary of the October Revolution, I wonder about the propaganda value of this picture. Surely, the film wasn't made to glorify the "heroic sacrifices" of the Red Army. If this movie shows anything, it reveals the brutality, the stupidity and terrifying contingency of war through the ingenious ideas and compelling camera work of Miklós Jancsó, one of the significant figures of modern Hungarian cinema.

History or Novel? Laurent Binet's "HHhH"

When I was in Montreal shortly after Christmas, I visited the Gallimard bookstore to browse around and buy at least one French novel. The first book that caught my attention had not only an odd title but also an unusual illustration on its cover. It showed the peaked cap and the uniform of a high-ranking SS officer without the face of this mysterious personage.

When I glanced at the title all that I found were a series of letters, *"HHhH"* of which at first, I couldn't make any sense. Only when I looked again at the blurb in the back of this French paperback did it become clear to me that these letters stood for two top Nazis, Heinrich Himmler and Reinhard Heydrich. In fact, as I discovered later, the series of "H"s actually mean "Himmlers brain is called Heydrich" *("Hitlers Hirn heisst Heydrich").*

I also found out that this was a novel by Laurent Binet, a French lycée teacher whose book won the prestigious Prix Goncourt for a first novel. As I am a fan of historical fictions, especially those set during the Second World War, I picked up the book and started to read it as soon as I had a chance to do so.

To my surprise this is no ordinary novel, but a mixture of historical narratives interspersed with continuous comments of the author about the idiosyncratic way he is trying to make sense of the most dramatic secret undertakings of the last war, the assassination of Reinhard Heydrich, the greatly feared and devilishly clever Nazi Protector of German occupied Bohemia and Moravia. As I went on reading *"HHhH,"* I became increasingly aware that I had found myself in the workshop of a novelist haunted by the circumstances of Heydrich's assassination that took place in Prague in May, 1942.

Even though he soaked up anything he could find out about Himmler's most powerful associate and about those who managed to kill him, Binet is full of doubts about whether he could ever do justice to his subject. What he is, in fact, trying to do is straddle the often very thin line dividing the novelist from the historian. There is no doubt both have a story to tell, but when do they fail if they overstep each others' supposed boundaries? Is history so inexhaustible and its details ultimately so concealed that the historian and especially the novelist cannot but invent stories to produce a coherent narrative?

Is Binet perhaps overdramatizing his undertaking when he writes, "When I say that to invent a character to understand the facts of history, it is as if you would put makeup on the [historical] evidence?" This is a question which, if taken seriously, could give rise to complex epistemological debates among theoreticians of history. Fortunately, Binet, who after all is trying a novel - which he once pointedly calls an "infra novel" - has no intention of tormenting his readers with such nit-picking arguments. What I believe is that he only suggests in a metaphorical way that trying to fill in the details of history is much more problematic than most people would imagine.

This is especially true as far as the assassination of Heydrich is concerned, for as one historian has observed, "He is widely recognized as one of the great iconic villains of the twentieth century." No wonder that this gruesome and feared collaborator of Himmler has been portrayed as the embodiment of the arch-Nazi in popular culture. Hollywood movies like Douglas Sirk's *"Hitler's Madman"* or Fritz Lang's *"Hangmen also Die"* had set the tone for this widespread mythical representation. It is precisely this kind of highly fictionalized and higher than life image that prompts Binet to tread very carefully in trying to create a credible and coherent account of the historical events that culminated in Heydrich's assassination.

What I find particularly striking in *"HHhH"* is Binet's almost obsessive ways of struggling with his material, for his novel reads at times like a personal diary showing how his project progresses. He mentions, for instance, his numerous visits to Prague which he hopes will set the atmosphere of the city on the day when the assassination took place. At other times he is seen to be engaged in conversations with persons who know about his projects and whose criticism he considers as important. He is especially aware of the negative comments about his ongoing work, like those of his girlfriend who is startled by Himmler's imagined reaction on learning about the crash of the fighter aircraft that Heydrich was piloting himself:

"What do you mean," she exclaims to her friend, "by 'the blood rising to his cheeks?' 'His brain is swelling in his cranial box'? But you are simply fantasizing, aren't you?"

Despite these compunctions, Binet cannot help inventing scenes which are meant to illuminate the characters of the leading figures in *"HHhH."* While there is nothing strange about these kinds of "animations," reading history as a novel make the reader reflect on the imaginative license of an author who is so much aware of the thin line that separates the historical evidence from telling a story. Surprisingly, he once recklessly oversteps this delicate boundary by imagining that he himself is asleep in the catacombs of the Greek Orthodox Church in the compartments reserved for the dead monks, in the church which becomes the ultimate refuge of the parachutists who were sent to kill Heydrich. What I find much more convincing are the counter-factual speculations interspersed in the novel. Would the Holocaust, of which he was one of the chief architects, have lost some of its deadly effects if he had continued to serve in the Navy as a career officer? The author suggests that if Heydrich hadn't been court martialled and thrown out from the Navy for unbecoming conduct, he would probably never have found his way to his patron Heinrich Himmler whose "brain" and most fanatical acolyte he became.

Speculative questions like these call for a more thorough understanding of Heydrich's career and character. Reading Binet's novel I was prompted to turn to the latest biography of this frighteningly powerful Nazi who has had a hand in a great many plots and murderous campaigns of the Third Reich. In reading Robert Gerwath's *"Hitler's Hangman. The Life of Heydrich,"* I am beginning to see much clearer what an evil genius this man was. There is no doubt that he was an exceptionally gifted individual. Talented musician, champion fencer, excellent sportsman, pilot and above all a superb organizer, he devoted his life to conceiving and helping carry out the most depraved projects of the Third Reich. Apart from Goebbels, he was the most sinister and effective key official of Hitler's Germany. To enable the regime to exert as much terror as possible, he completely reorganized the Reich Security Service (the so called SD) which he then streamlined with the Gestapo. As a result, he had the means to utilize both of these dreaded organizations for his own dangerous intrigues and sinister purposes. Heydrich was also the one who convened and also presided over the Wannsee Conference in which the implementation of the "Final Solution" of the Jews under the Third Reich was coordinated. What's more, as the consummation of these preparatory measures, he organized the special task-forces, the so called *"Einsatzgruppen"* who carried out the gigantic massacres in Poland and the occupied areas of the Soviet Union. And as the climax of his ultra-rapid career, he became in 1941 the acting Reich Protector of Bohemia and Moravia.

There are good reasons why Hedyrich had become a special target for the British as the all powerful ruler of the Czech Protectorate. For he didn't only largely suppress the resistance movements in these strategically important territories. What's worse, he also managed to increase the armaments production of the huge Skoda works for the benefit of the Wehrmacht by a clever carrot-and-stick policy. Worried as well as irritated by the conditions in that occupied country, the British Secret Services in conjunction with the Czechoslovak government in-exile organized the "Anthropoid" mission which resulted in the elimination of one of the highest ranking Nazi officials. However, there still remain doubts as to whether this coup was really worthwhile considering the dreadful price paid for it by the Czech population. In revenge, the Nazis wrought terrible terror, killing thousands of people and wiping out the village of Lidice with most of its inhabitants. Gerwarth makes an interesting point when he observes that, "Through his death, Heydrich inadvertently fulfilled one of his short-term missions in Prague: the complete and lasting 'pacification' of the Protectorate."

It is one of the merits of Laurent Binet's *"HHhH"* that he manages to convey many of the events and concerns relating to Heydrich's career and assassination. Even though his book is an experiment of an amateur historian struggling with methodological issues and historical uncertainties, it appears that his '"infra novel" has found many readers who until the appearance of this unusual quasi-historical, quasi-literary account, haven't had any serious interest in this heroic and tragic story.

Remembering Virginia

Note. *Rummaging through my papers I came across two emails describing the last days and the death of a very dear friend Virginia B. She had terminal cancer and she had one of her arms amputated during the last phases of her illness. Despite her handicap, she continued as long as she could in her job as a very much loved, specially trained, high school teacher. When she died earlier than expected "outracing our best guesses, even allowing for a generous denial factor," as her brother put it, on hearing the news, I sat down and wrote him the following letter which was read at the memorial service for her on July 19, 2008.*

There has not been a day since I learnt of Virginia's death that I haven't been trying to capture her image which, I must say, had somewhat faded while our contacts had stopped due to her illness. Strange as it is, now that she is dead, memories keep stirring in me which had never surfaced while she was alive.

I suddenly remember details of the day six years ago when we spent hours looking at Monet's wonderful canvasses at the *Musée Marmottan* in Paris. I recall in particular her perceptive comments on the painter's marvellously atmospheric *"Train in Winter,"* a framed copy of which now hangs in our apartment. I also suddenly remember how she struggled on, despite her aching knees on an absurdly long walk from our hotel to Notre Dame during a scorching day in July. While it would have been saner to have taken refuge under the shady trees of the *Jardin du Luxembourg*, we both felt that we had to take that long walk because that was her last day in Paris.

The last time I saw Virginia was two years ago when she invited me to stay with her in Tacoma after she had learnt that I was to spend a week with my wife's sister and her husband in Victoria, BC. She came to meet me with her niece at the docks of Port Angeles from where we drove first to her mother's house near Puget Sound. It was there that I got acquainted with that remarkably sprightly, witty old lady.

My mind is filled with pictures and fragments of the conversations during the days I spent in Virginia's company in and around Tacoma. Thanks to her, I got an insider's view of that marvellously picturesque region of the United States which I had never seen before. I have also the most pleasant memories of the few days that I spent as her guest in her spacious, very comfortable house. One of the highlights of those days was our phone conversation with our mutual friend, Susan A. who lives in Sydney, Australia.

Virginia, Susan and I got to know one another in “Table Talk”, one of the best known forums of the Internet. We were both attracted by Virginia’s playful and charming style which, to me at least, was entirely new in online forums. We were drawn to each other by an elective affinity which was reflected by the emails which we exchanged with one another. We playfully envisaged meeting sometime in Australia, though we knew that nothing would come of this project. It was therefore all the more exciting when Virginia and I spoke on the phone with Susan one afternoon from Tacoma. I felt that this memorable conversation would only strengthen our friendship, and I secretly fancied that Virginia and I may still make it one day to Sydney, Australia.

Things have turned out entirely differently from what I have hoped for. Virginia is no longer with us. Yet she is still very much alive in me as someone who inspired me to cultivate a friendship which was especially meaningful and entirely different from any that I ever had.

www.ingramcontent.com/pod-product-compliance
Lightning Source LLC
LaVergne TN
LVHW010913110826
845149LV00013B/2349

* 9 7 8 0 9 8 7 1 6 7 5 7 6 *